MW01596592

COLORING THE ALPHABET

AN ABCEDRIAN SOURCE BOOK

If you make a copy of a page, you and your father can color it together. That works with friends, too!

Rev. Gretchen A.L. Schork, MA, OCL:AL

First two for each letter are traditional,
The First is on a DIAPER ◇ pattern, and
           it is a Blackletter shape
The Second is a VERSAL letter
Both of these are from the "Middle Ages", before
           the Rennaisance.
Next is an optical illusion, sort of like the Neo-
           Impressionism of the 20th century.

**A Project by
SIAPress Buffalo**

**For
Lulu.com**

The cartoon is my idea— something "crazy" to make
    the letters into personalities , I colored them and they
are going up online at Facebook.com / Meeting the Letters
    At B are up now, I am adding a new one in alternate weeks.

ISBN 978-1-71688-298-2

Publisher: Lulu.com

Production by
SIAPress Buffalo
P O Box 304
Buffalo, NY 14215

A IS FOR ACTION AND AWAKE

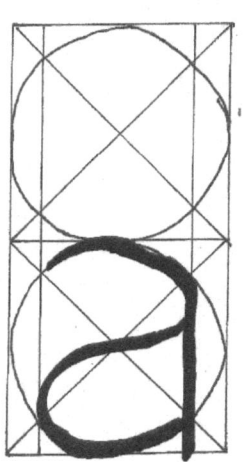

AWAKE!

Wake up! There is a whole new book to be colored! Get to play!

Here are over 100 pages of letters that can be colored! It will be fun, so what are you waiting for?!

ACTION.

To wake up and have fun, we are inviting you to take action. Pick up your markers or your pencils, and start coloring you like.

ASTER

Family: Daisy (Compositae)

This is the Latin name for a large group of wildflowers. They grow mostly in fields, and bloom in the fall. Their flowers are white, lavender or violet, and are shaped like a star.

A field of asters will look like there is a fog of color: the deep violet ones will tickle the eyes because they are so deeply colored.

It is hard to know which Aster you are looking at: they have differences in the arrangement oaf the flowers, and the shape of the leaves. But all of them have the small, star-like flower that gives them their names.

When you see Asters, it is time to go back to school, the leaves will be turning soon, and crisp fall is in the air. Even when they bloom before the first frost, they are so associated with fall that they will cool the eye and echo with the memory of early snowflakes from a grey sky.

A is associated with the idea of Spirit, the part of us that allows us to connect with the greater Spirit that we can call the Source, the Universe, or even for some, Deity. It is part of us, and helps us connect to the very best that we can be.

The symbol for Spirit is two triangles. This is an overlap of the other four elemental symbols, for Earth, Air, Fire and Water.

Make this design black and white checkerboard to keep the symbol and the letter flashing back and forth between the two.

Or you can use two colors that are complements: red and green; blue and orange; or yellow and violet.

The idea of this technique is "flashing letters." The optical illusion makes your eyes bounce back and forth between the letter and the symbol. By using complementary colors, the "flashing" is made even more apparent. Complements vibrate in a design like this. The more solid the colors, the better the flashing effect will be. Look for color suggestions in any of the letters of this book.

Red, green	red-orange, blue-green
Blue, orange	red-violet, yellow-green
Yellow, violet	blue-violet, yellow-orange

"You know, all these flowers are part of the world. They know their place in the Universe, and I am happy to say, that place is here! Each one is a singular beauty."

You look again at the flowers, and realize that they are, indeed, individual plants, each in its own patch of ground, sometimes only an inch square, other times larger for the larger plants.

"But each one is part of the whole garden, too. They are a collective of beauty, all one in how they harmonize into the whole display. They make a beautiful garden."

Now you see the whole display together. No longer individual plants, te whole is a vibrant ecosystem of living beings. Bees and flowers and moss and grasshoppers, all needed to complete the wholeness of the garden. Together they synthesize a collective scent that is a perfume of beauty. You inhale it deeply, eyes closed to concentrate on the aroma.

"And when you see this garden, it is part of the whole hillside, too, and all the different experiences that are part of it. You can think of the whole hill as one place, one garden of plants and animals living together."

"Let's take an even bigger view. This hill is part of a continent, vast and living. And then, the continent is part of the panet Earth, the big blue ball in space. And then you can feel the planet Earth in orbit with the Moon, traveling about the Sun, and then the place of the Sun in the Milky Way. And the Milky Way as a single galaxy in the vastness of space with all the other galaxies that make up the universe."

"And this, the entire Universe, lives inside you, just as you are inside it. There is no division between you and the nebula, or between the star and your ability to see it."

B IS FOR BOUNTY AND BONDING.

BOUNTY

Bless with as much as can be handled, and then a little more. It is a feeling within that accepts the gift with gratitude.

BONDING

Bring both parties into a relationship that lasts through time or trouble, helping both to have companionship on the road of life.

BERRIES

Family: Rose (Rosaceae)

Genus: Rubus

Raspberries, Blackberries, Thimbleberries, and all the other rambling bushes of berry are included in this group.

Berries brighten the bush, inviting the birds and deer and other animals (including us!) to pick them and eat them. They are (mostly) delicious precursors to future bushes.

When a berry bush is planted by a bird (when they, you know, do that thing), it will eventually take over the area. They spread with their prickles and insist on taking new ground.

B is the letter for Venus, round and soft on one side, but solid and strong on the other. It is the planet associated with attraction: not only to a mate, but to friends, community, groups that work together to foster a better future. All the beauty of nature is included in the ideas associated with Venus.

The traditional symbol for Venus is round, like the womb that is crucible for the formation of new life, and positive, with the combination of male (-) and female (+) in perfect balance.

Make this design black and white checkerboard to keep the symbol and the letter flashing back and forth between the two.

Or, use the green of Venus, contrasting with red to make it vibrate.

Or, make the background green, with the symbol and letter segments in black and white.

"We have been expecting you! Bright Blessings be yours." As she moves, small flowers sprout in her wake. It is an odd sight, but lends to her beauty.

"Be at peace here. Share in our bounty. Rest if you will, sit with us and let your hands weave the flowers into a bower for sleep."

You notice that one group next to where you stand have been weaving flowers taken from large baskets. They are making wreaths and chains of flowers as they sing in unison. One of the weavers stands up and puts a circle of the flowers around your neck.

"The afternoon wanes, and soon the fireflies will be with us. They are such joyous creatures! But no, you are a traveler. You have to move on, yes?"

You nod, and so does B. "Well, then, let us offer you a bit of food before you move on."

As you taste the food, more than food passes into you. The feeling is like being flooded from top to bottom by a soothing and healing flame. It is warm and cleansing. And it seems to have ethereal qualities that are the concentrated nature of fire, yet it does not burn. You are refreshed, and you feel a drive to make a positive impact on life and growth in your own life no matter that the feeling has no form, no focus you can find that later, when you think about the letter B

C IS FOR CREATING AND CHANGING.

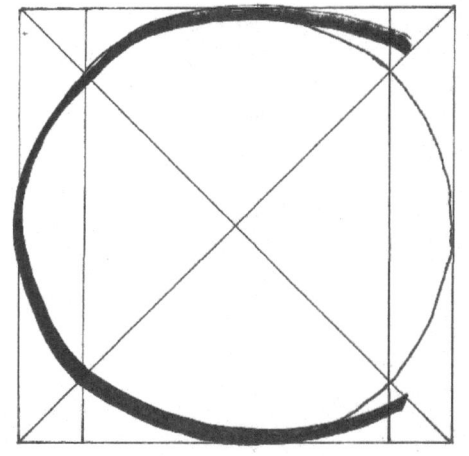

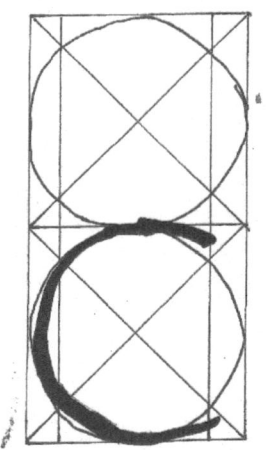

CREATING

Be creative! Combine two or more things, not always related, in a way that forces a new thing, concept, or result.

CHANGING

Make new creations, make changes to the old, and makes the creation into a new reality.

CAMPION

Family: Pinka (Caryophyllacaea)
Genus: Silene
Bladder Campion: Silene nivea
Campion has calyx sacks that look a bit like a miniature white melon. They look improbable, catching the eye in gravelly areas. They are usually white. Their family is Silene, a word that reminds the observant of Selene, the Moon Goddess.

They bloom in very early summer in gravelly areas. Because the leaves are not large, they tend to be overlooked. But the bladder makes them unique, and fun to find.

The Bladder Campion is an alien species, which means it came here from Europe. It likes the soils and sun in the north east, so it decided to stay.

C stands for the Moon, whose symbol is a crescent, just like the C. This one is easy to see and remember.

The Moon waxes and wanes, and pulls water into the tides that ebb and flow. Since we are 70% or so water, the Moon pulls on us too. Nothing ever stays the same when the Moon is involved.

Make this design black and white checkerboard to keep the symbol and the letter flashing back and forth between the two.

Or, the background can be violet, or purple, with black and white segments.

Or, use lavender for the background, and violet and yellow for the symbol and letter segments.

Iridescent colors are appropriate, since the Moon's light can be magical.

There are many shades of violet and purple that can be used, just as there are many yellows. Try to choose colors that are matched in intensity and opposite in brightness.

"Greetings, Traveler! It is good you have reached me now, for the Moon is only bright for part of the night, and her cycle is nearly half spent."

"You can create a lot, should you choose to visit here often. Come dream with me! Look deep into your own mind, to the hidden places, dream with me, and you will generate wonderful things!"

She is moving around the clearing, graceful as a ballerina, surrounded by fireflies that resemble stars glittering around and through her fancy dress. It is hard to look away. Her voice becomes even softer. "Or you can stay with me, and we will glory in the mystery of the night, the warm rays of the Moon will be our lantern."

That strikes you as strange, because the Moon's light is cold, not warm art all. There is a fluttering of wings, and the guardian of the Moon lands beside you.

"Excuse me, Madame C, this child is under my care. There is precious little time to waste here, if you don't mind my saying so."

C is not happy, and straightens up, stiffens, and makes a sound similar to a "harrumph". The spell has been broken, the awareness of the need to move is renewed. You bow slightly, and then continue on your way.

D IS FOR DEPENDABLE AND DRIVE.

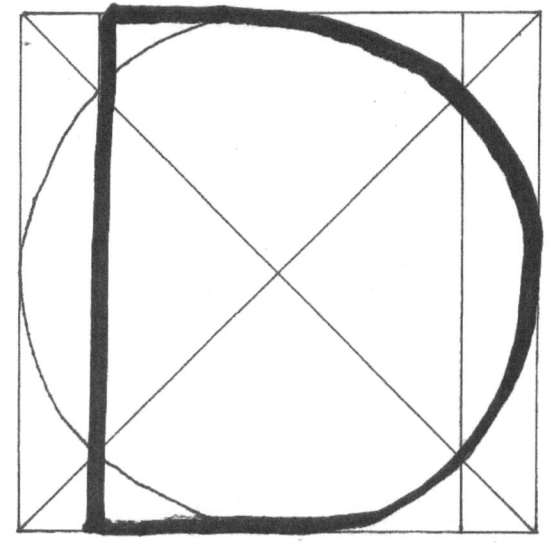

DEPENDABLE

When behavior or characteristics are both known and consistent, and can be relied on.

DRIVE

It's what carries effort forward toward a goal, and works better when the goal is deliberate and chosen.

DOGWOOD

Family: Dogwood (Cornaceae)

Genus: Cornus

Dogwood is a small tree (Cornus amomum, Flowering Dogwood bush) or an herb called Cornus canadensis, Dwarf Cornel, or Bunchberry.

The tree has delicate flowers in a soft tint of pale pink, early in the spring, and it is used for landscaping. When found in the wild, it appears like a slight mist or speckles on the spring green. The flowers are about two inches with four petals.

The herb likes acid soil, and is found in boggy areas. It also has four petals, and only grows to six or eight inches. It does not gather in groups, so is easy to miss.

D is associated with Taurus, the celestial bull. The dates for Taurus are April 22 to May 20.

The symbol for Taurus is a circle head with two horns. This looks like the head of a bull or cow. On the D itself, it looks like this symbol turned on its side.

Make this design black and white checkerboard to keep the symbol and the letter flashing back and forth between the two.

Or, the color for Taurus is red-orange. The compliment is blue-green. So these two colors can be used for the letter and symbol segments.

Or, you can use the red-orange as a background for the black and white checkerboard on the letter and symbol.

Because this letter uses tertiary colors (the ones mixing the primary and secondary colors), you can use a wide range of colors for each of the two named. Blue-green can be turquoise, aqua, teal, or any variation on those colors. That gives you a lot of choices for coloring this letter and symbol!

"You like that stone? Keep it. We have plenty to share. A pocket stone helps hold memory of where it came from. And it is solid. That is what I like about this place: it is solid. Nothing is more solid than this. Nice, straight-forward solid forms. they are satisfying in so many ways."

"I value their solidity. Keeps me grounded. Being flighty or air headed, well, that is just not my style. Here, look at this one." D approaches a large slab set against another block so it stands up. "Amazing work, the way the workmen have made it slim, but it is still strong."

"These blocks are my friends. Now, they are not my relatives or close friends, because they are all going to be shipped within a week. But they are still friends. I keep notes on the shapes and sizes of the blocks. It is lie giving them a name, letting them be real, so to speak. The record is a solid thing that preserves the memory of their being here at one time in their stony lives. You have to know who and what is important to you. Make the relationship solid as rock. For all that you carve and refine the block and the relationship, it is still a living thing. These rocks help think solid thoughts."

"Have you ever met a living rock? No? Well, maybe you have but did not know it. Look at that rock you put in your pocket."

"It is a living rock. It is a living creature. No! Really! I mean it! It doesn't move on its own, I will grant you that. No, it needs a glacier, a stream or a person to move it. But deep within, it is alive with rock-life. Try to sense that life, and see how it is different than your life. Make that stone your friend. It will always be there for you. You know part of its origin story now. You will be part of its life story, too, as long as you keep it and occasionally think about it, and hold it."

E IS FOR EXPANSIVE AND EXPLORATION.

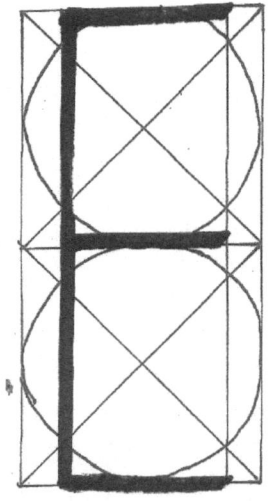

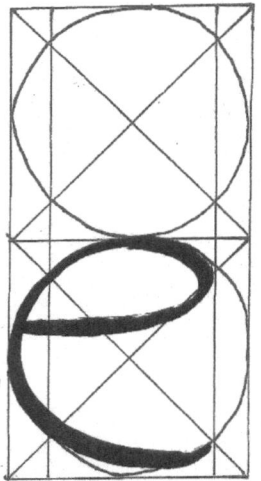

EXPANSIVE

Big energy fills all the available space. Just like E, Air, it moves but is not seen.

EXPLORATION

Checking out every possibility is not possible, but more than first thought can lead to new ideas.

ELDERBERRY

Family: Adoxaceae
Genus: Sambucus
Elderberry is a bush whose berries can help with general health when made into a syrup. Flowers and berries grow in flat clusters.

The flowers are white, and are on a rather flat-topped stem. This makes them look very lacey on the bush. The flowering bush even looks like it will be healthy to know.

The berries are extremely deep purple, and can stain your clothing. They are made into a syrup for a general tonic to support the immune system, and for coughs.

The letter E is associated with the element of Air. This element is breezy, fresh, open and inviting in the early part of the day. But it can also be stifling, stale and hard to breathe. So we concentrate on the positive aspect, and try to fix the negative to be more inviting. That is why we have furnaces and air conditioners in our homes!

The symbol for Air is easy to remember. It is an A with a line closing the triangle at the bottom.

Color choices can include several combinations.

Make this design black and white checkerboard to keep the symbol and the letter flashing back and forth between the two.

Or, use the black and white pattern, with a yellow background.

Or, use yellow and violet on the letter and symbol segments.

Or, use a brilliant, intense yellow with a pale, light yellow. This will not flash. Instead, it will intrigue the eye and move in and out of focus.

Make copies of the design and try several combinations of colors. Then choose the one that you feel does the best job of making the letter and symbol show to best advantage.

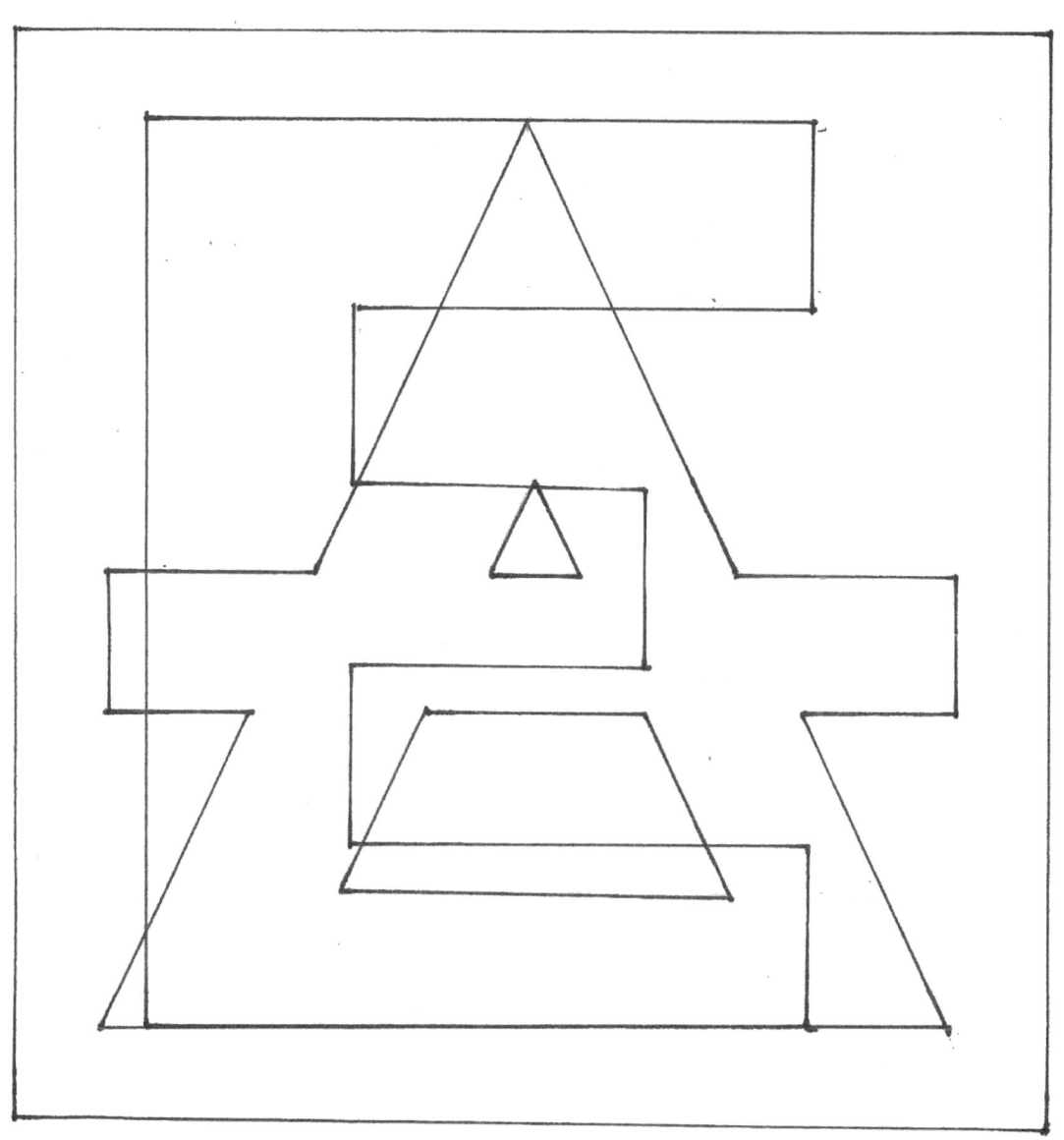

"Yes, well. So, the process of deciding things has many layers to be considered. So, you have to take responsibility for what you choose to do. But you also have to take responsibility for what you choose not to do. And here is the catch. If you do not make a choice, you have also made a choice. That means, of course, that you have to choose. No getting around that. You just do. Are you following me now?" You nod.

"Moving on. I create a box. (He gestures to make a square, then gestures to make sides and a top to the box.) Good. Now I have a box. It has perfect angles, because that is the concept I hold of a box. I can see the pattern of the angles and how the sides relate to the top and bottom."

He waives his hands to dismiss the image.

"Here we have a box, but (gesturing in a circle) it is no longer angled and squarish. If I stack several of these mind images together, I can draw a simple form of city scape. With more irregular forms, I can build a landscape. Like a painter, but much faster and more direct, I create an entire countryside. But if I do not commit the images to some form of physical media, they blow away with the wind, thus." He blows on the image, and it apparently dissipates like a fog.

"I build images of concepts in my mind, or in my mind's eye. Depends on how you want to consider it. That image is a pattern that carries symbolic relationship to the image my physical eyes would see if I were to look at the original landscape that the image represents."

"This is what we do here. We wiggle ideas and concepts around to organize thinking into some sort of sensible order. That makes it easier to pass instructions on to our hands or assistants."

F IS FOR FERVOR AND FORCE.

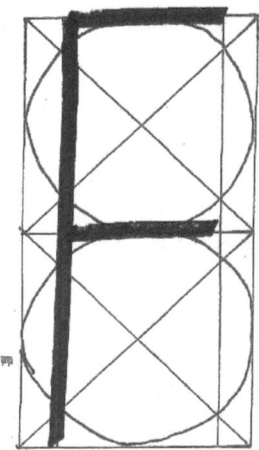

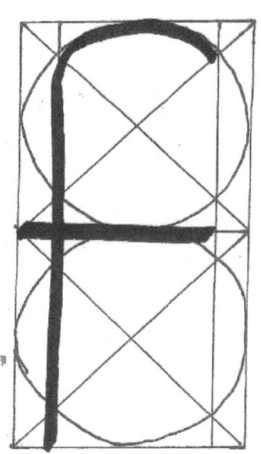

FERVOR

When you desire something deeply enough to work hard to get it, and you continue to work hard as time passes and the results are delayed, that is called fervor. It is an abiding desire to reach a goal, no matter what has to be overcome in the process of attaining it.

FORCE

Push hard toward goals with all you have. Reach deep inside to find more energy and strength: that is force in action. But the force has to be applied in a way that will give the results you are looking for. Otherwise, the force is wasted.

FOXGLOVE

Family: Snapdragon (Scrophulariaceae)

Genus: Penstemon digitalis

This one is called Foxglove Beardtongue. It grows in fields and other waste places, but is not common. The flower is white with stamens that look like a hairy tongue sticking out. Do NOT use this plant for medicine: it is powerful, and in its natural state will kill you. It is related to the source of digitalis, the heart medicine. If it is not treated the right way, you will not know how strong the dose is, and you will probably overdose with it. There is great wisdom in knowing the difference between "this is where the medicine comes from" and "I can use this now."

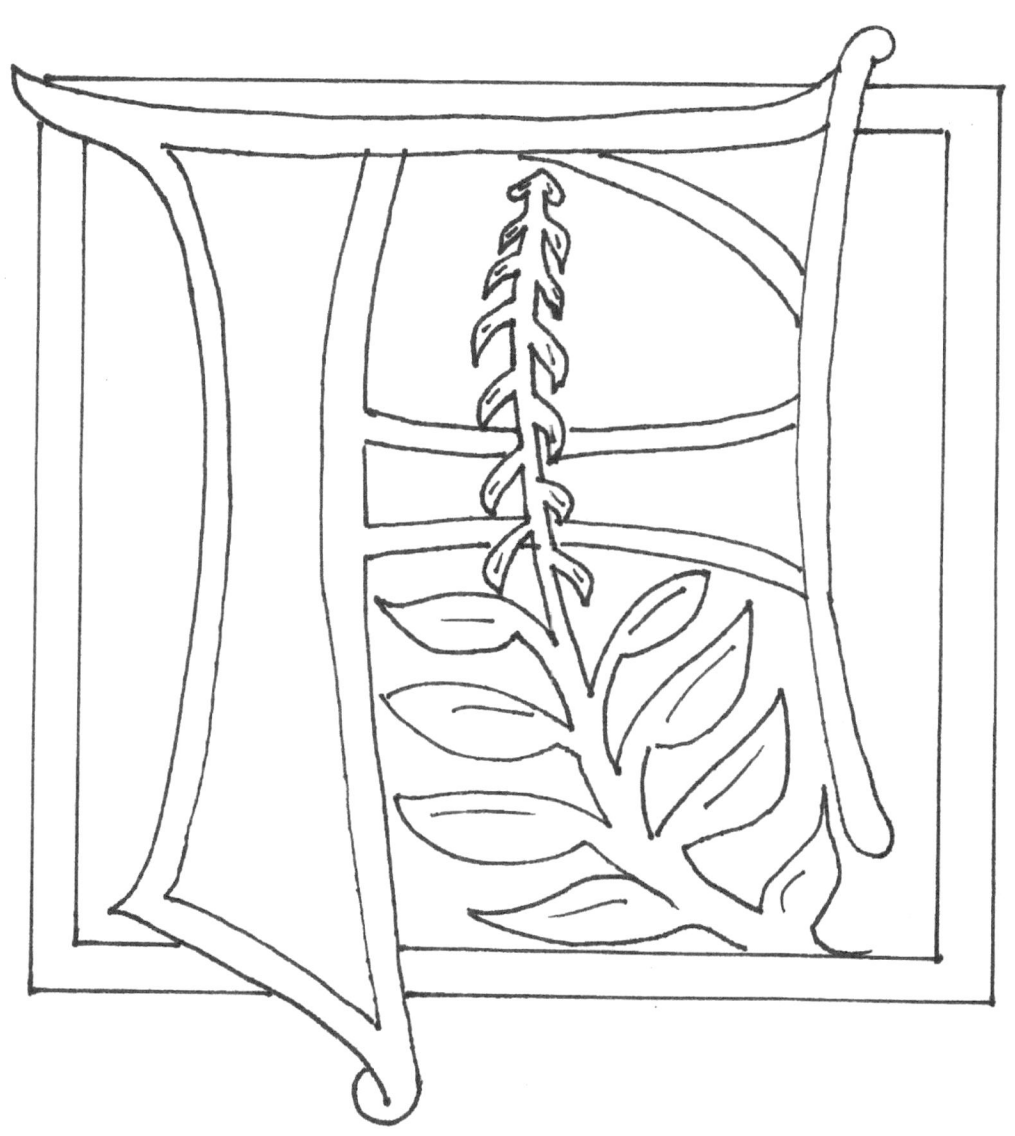

The letter F is associated with the planet Mars. This is the strong and forceful planet of the warrior and the blacksmith, both of whom harness their strength in service of a greater good.

The symbol for Mars is a circle, which reminds us of the circle of life, with an arrow that is like the spear of the warrior. When being positive, the spear serves the whole of the life cycle, which means the warrior guards and protects the whole community. We will leave the negative aspects aside for now.

The color choices are brilliant for this combination. Try one or more of the following ideas.

Make this design black and white checkerboard to keep the symbol and the letter flashing back and forth between the two.

Or, put an intense red in the background of the black and white pattern.

Or, use a deep red and a bright red, with no background color.

Or, use red and green for the letter and symbol segments. You might try black or white for the background.

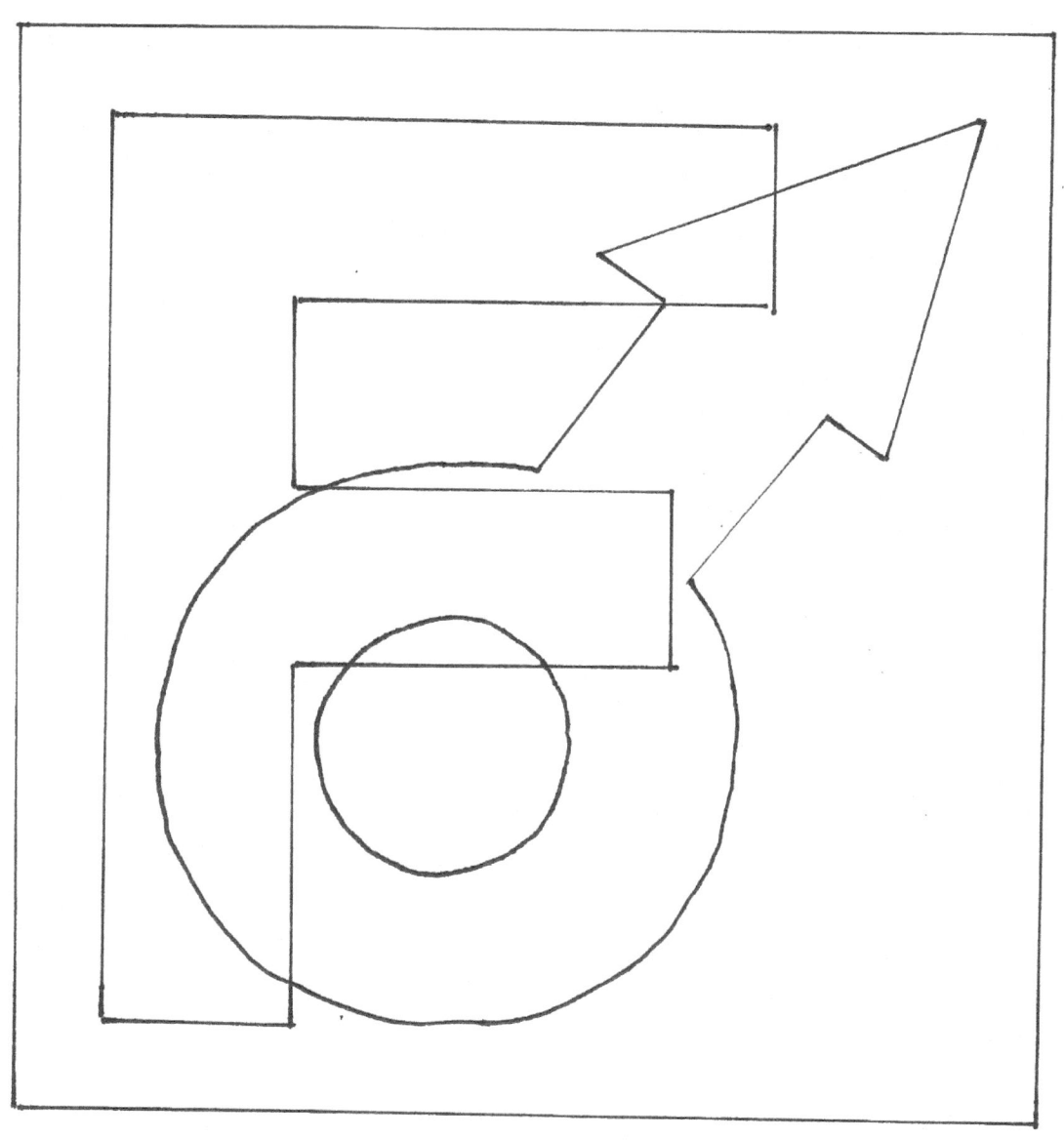

"So, here is a lesson for you. This is very important, so pay attention, and always remember what I have said."

"These two swords are both weapons. They are perfect killing machines, each in their own way. Do you hear me? They are for KILLING. Well, maiming and killing, actually, but not to quibble. They KILL. That is what they are made for. The sun out there kills too. But the sun does not target. It just burns everything. So, we have three weapons."

"This is a plow blade. It can kill too. Not made to, but can kill. It is supposed to make growing plant things easier. This one has an especially sharp blade. Yes, sharp enough to kill. Handy fact to know."

"So, lots of ways to kill. You can kill with a properly made pen, too. But the point is, WHY?" The pause pulls at you.

"Killing is how you eat. You kill to live. You can never get away from that. Kill the deer. Kill the rabbit. Kill the wheat. Kill. Kill. Kill. Everything that lives has to kill to keep living."

He walks away, then comes back. "When you kill, use the right tool, and kill swiftly without pain. Or as little pain as you can manage. Never waste what you kill, if you can help it. Better to choose the weapon you will use so it will do an efficient job. Now, here is another weapon to kill with." He holds up a surgical scalpel blade, examining it carefully.

"This blade will kill a tumor that is trying to kill you. So, it is defensive. Kill it before it kills you. Self-defense. Rather elegant, isn't it?"

"This plow blade sometimes kills small animals in the field that is being plowed. That is accidental killing. Still kills, but not on purpose. That is a different kind of killing."

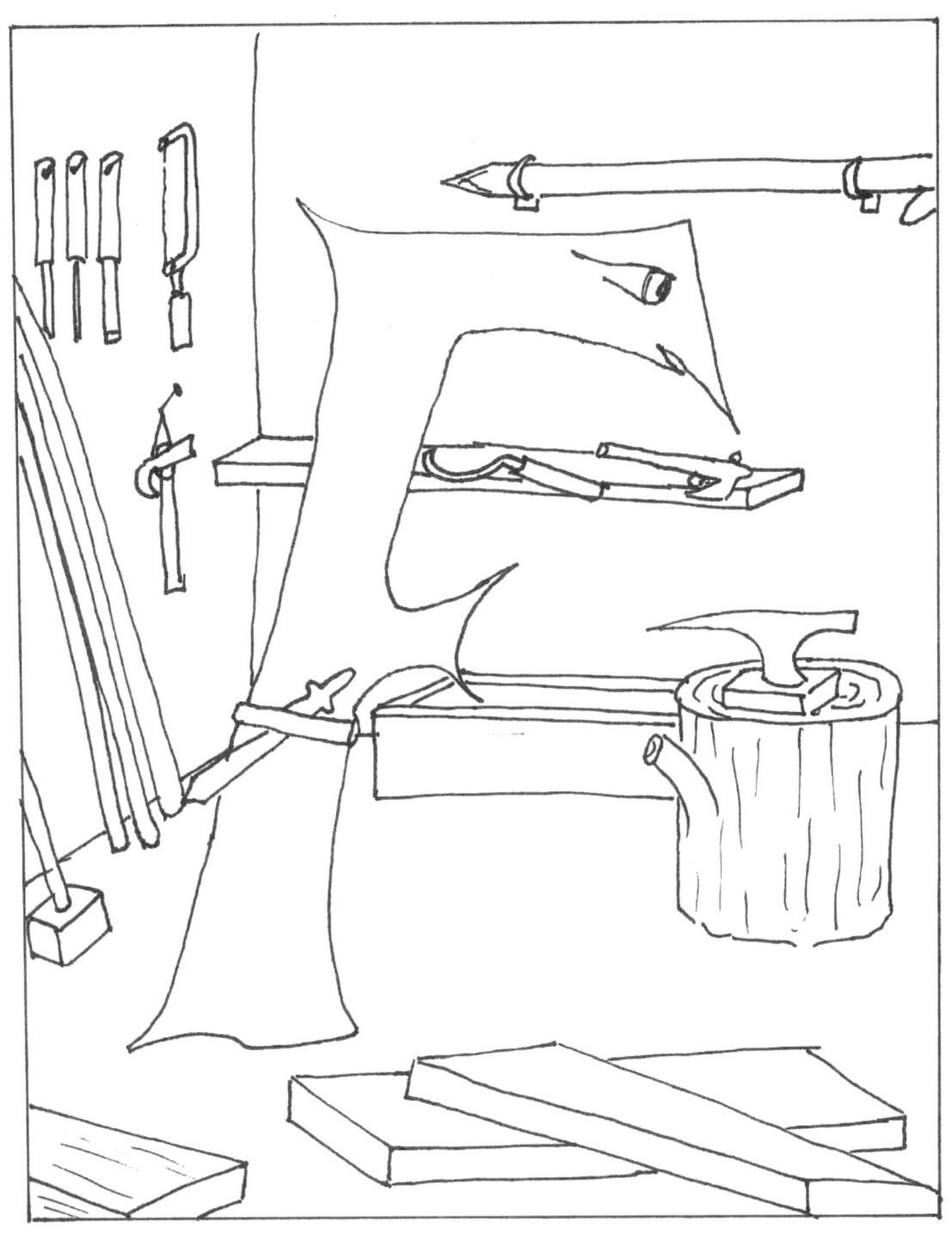

G IS FOR GROWTH AND GUARDING.

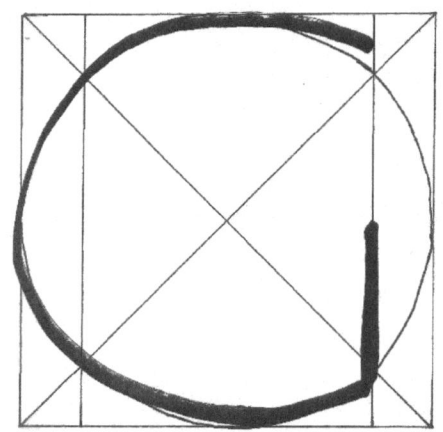

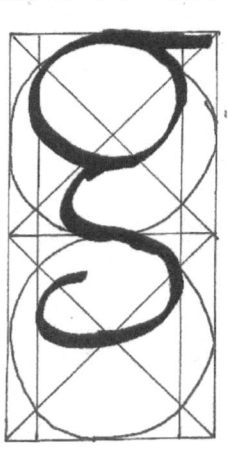

GROWTH

Work with your goals as if they were flowers in a garden. They will require watering to nourish them and make them grow. Your goals will need weeding, to be sure you don't get distracted by side projects.

GUARDING

That all requires an attitude of guarding the seed: nourish, protect, encourage: these are the steps that will help you get to your goals more often and with less distraction.

GIANT TRILLIUM,

Family: Lily (Liliaceae)

Genus: Trillium grandiflorum

This flower can be identified from a car on a super highway: it is showy and brilliant against the dark, damp earth of spring. It has a three pattern: three leaves, three petals. There is usually one flower per one leaf.

This is the major find of spring: it is beautiful, almost glowing in the sunshine that filters through hardwood trees that have not yet fully sprouted their leaves.

The petals will fade to a delicate pink. If you find deep red flowers, it is Wakerobin, or Red Trillium. The Sesil trillium has no distance between the flower and the leaf.

Trillium is hard to grow in a garden, but well worth it. Please buy the plants from a reputable company: they are protected by federal law in the wild.

The letter G is associated with Cancer, the crab constellation of the Zodiac. Its dates ae June 21 to July 22.

The symbol for Cancer is the claws of the crab, open and crossed in front of the crab. Keep in mind that some symbols take a little imagination to see the meaning that is intended.

The color choices can include the following.

Make this design black and white checkerboard to keep the symbol and the letter flashing back and forth between the two.

Or, use the black and white pattern on the letter and symbol segments, with yellow-orange for the background.

Or, use yellow-orange and blue-violet for the letter and symbol segments, with white for the background. You can use black, but it will probably not go well with the dark nature of the blue-violet.

Or, use the yellow-orange and blue-violet for the segments, and a lilac or pale violet for the background. This is the color of the Moon, which is the plant that rules the constellation of Cancer.

Or, do the same pair of colors, with a background of medium or light blue. This is the color of the element Water that is part of the nature of Cancer, a Water sign.

We are adding more ways to pick colors. By now you may have figured out that there are two approaches: first, you can use symbolic color on the design; or second, you can choose colors that satisfy your own taste and preferences.

The colors suggested are just that: suggestions. The coloring is yours, so the colors are chosen by you!

"You have to know, though, that control is not all it is cracked up to be! Oh, no, indeed! Sometimes you have to let go, just feel it all, all at once, and let the feelings surge. That is how you take care of yourself, you know. And if you do not take care of yourself, you will never be able to help take care of anyone else. That would be a tragedy! A true tragedy! You care about that, yes?"

Before you can actually nod agreement, G continues. "There is a flexibility that is needed in all matters of nurturing. It's a thin line between being indecisive, which is too much flexibility, and rigidity, which is too little flexibility. You are too smart to miss what I am saying. It is so obvious. Never mind, you will remember it in time."

"Then sometimes you may be caught up in your memories. Now, that is not a bad thing. Memories give value to our time spent in life, and that is a good to add into our personal treasury. But you can get caught in too much time thinking on what you already know, and it will blind you. That would be being stuck in the past. Or, if you forget what you know, you get blinded, and lose all the benefit of what you have gone through and learned already. It is always the middle way that you want. Not too much of a good thing, but not too little, either!"

"And then, there are the memories that you don't remember yet, because they have not yet happened. Or they were a dream, and you never expected them to be a reality for you. Those are the memories that I treasure the most! Oh! The things I have not yet remembered into my life! They are so exciting!"

H IS FOR HARMONY AND HIDING.

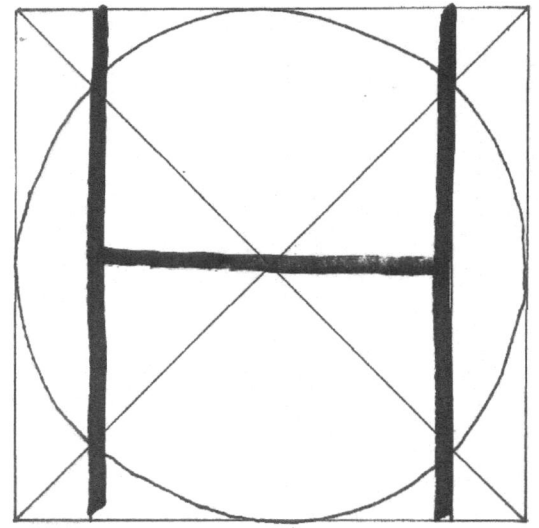

HARMONY

When coloring, it is easy to forget all the troubles of life, and focus on the color, the shape, and the feel of the pencil on the paper. That is a wonderful form of harmony: being at one with the process that you are doing, not worrying about anything. It helps clear the mind.

HIDING

Sometimes it is good to hide away our worries. They will be there for us when we finish taking a break. And perhaps they will be easier to handle when we have taken a brief rest. The key is, if you hide things away, remember where you put them, and get them out again later.

HEPATICA

Family: Buttercup (Ranunculaceae)
Genus: Hepatica acutiloba
The word, Hepatica, refers to the liver-like shape of the leaves. It is a spring flower with hairy stems to help with the cold nights of early spring. If you get it going in your spring garden, (buy the plants from a reputable nursery, they are protected) they can be a real delight before any other plants start up. The leaves remain all summer and winter, although they get rather worn out by the time new ones come up in the spring.

If you find a patch in the wild, come back each year to visit them. It makes for a delightful spring walk, and there are probably lots of other wild flowers to see in the same woods.

The letter H is associated with the Source of Life, or the Universe. This is very abstract, and rather spiritual. Think of the breath, when you do not use your voice. It can feel like you are breathing something very important when you do that.

The symbol for the Universe is a simple drawing of a bar or spiral galaxy. This is the largest unit of astronomy that we can imagine easily in our minds. Of course, we live in the Milky Way Galaxy, which therefore is our home. The idea is to look for a symbol that stands for something that is greater than we are, that we can never expect to become, no matter how hard we work at improving ourselves. A galaxy just about covers that idea.

Color choices can include the following.

Make this design black and white checkerboard to keep the symbol and the letter flashing back and forth between the two.

Or, use iridescent colors, if you have them, for the white, or for the background.

Iridescent tends to be very light with hints of colors that never really resolve into specific colors or shapes.it is like a pearly effect in a fog. Well, that comes close, but is still not quite the right colors. You can do all-pastel colors, if you wish, or a black background like the depths of space. Let the idea sit in your mind for a bit, and you will come up with a good idea. And as always, have fun with the process!

"We all work by the rules that have been set for us, long ago, before the universe came to be as we know it today. The Conductor is one of the beings who apply those rules to matter, so that the vibration will be harmonious. We will visit another of the Administrators of the Universe, one whose job is to make new stars. Her halls are quite impressive, but there is a lot of chaos in them. She specializes in drawing the chaos together so that it creates new star beings. I will go with you, but pay attention, my voice will not be heard in the confusion of her halls."

H rises from the ground, and you follow. Together you move through space toward a bright area, and as you get close, the formation begins to settle into patterns. "This is the Pillars of Creation[1], and the Star Maker works within. Hold onto my loop, my arm as you call it. Don't let go."

You do so, and are glad for the guidance. The vast nebula has several shafts, or Pillars, of dense matter that is glowing with energy and life.

As you approach, the small dots of light begin to resolve: they are baby stars, newly formed, beginning to pulse with life. H goes up to each one in turn and breathes into them. The Breath of Life makes them shine brighter, and with a rhythm of their own. The songs are loud in your mind, slightly off-tune, but resolving as they continue to sing.

I IS FOR IMAGINING AND INTEGRITY.

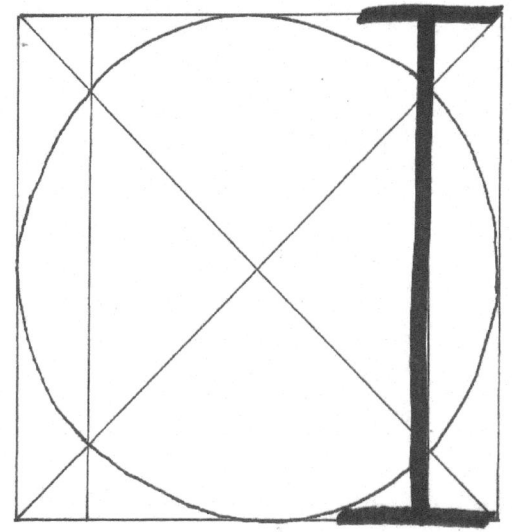

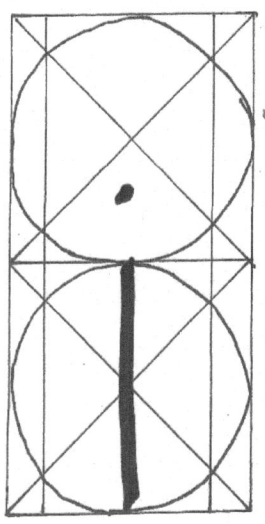

IMAGINING

What do you want, really? Can you dream it up, think it over, make it better, and then figure out what part you can work on to make it come into reality? See it, feel it, work for it.

INTEGRITY

It is easy to get distracted by momentary wants. But in the face of distractions, can you hold to what you believe, and what you consider to be a higher value? That is integrity. While you look ofr better ways in the world, can you keep a focus on what you hold to be valuable?

IMPATIENS

Family: Touch-me-not (Balsaminaceae)
Genus: Impatiens capensis
Common Name: Jewelweed

In the foolishness of my youth, when this letter was designed, the flower was not shown correctly. It should look like a snapdragon, but dangling from the stem. Sigh. So you are free to color as you wish, there is no realism involved.

The term Impatiens also applies to a domestic garden annual: it is also showy and colorful.

So, this letter has very little in scientific content to it. Now and then, the best system can break down!

The letter I is associated with the element of Water. Just as the water is deep or shallow, smooth or choppy, Water represents the changing emotions and feelings. It is the water in our bodies, the water we swim in, and the water of a falls.

The symbol for water is a triangle pointing down. This is the cup that the water settles down into when we pour it into the cup. It flows without effort, downward. In fact, it is hard to keep it from flowing.

Color choices all center around blue, in all its tints, shades, hues and mixes. Here are a few ideas.

Make this design black and white checkerboard to keep the symbol and the letter flashing back and forth between the two.

Or, use the black and white pattern with a blue background.

Or, make the blue background dark at the bottom and light at the top, shading it gradually from one to the other, without any dividing lines.

Or, use blue and orange for the letter and symbol segments, with a different blue in the background.

Or, play with the various blues that range from blue-green to blue-violet. But, only use one pair of colors on the letter and symbol segments. Otherwise, the pattern becomes confusing.

"Long journey, human? Thirsty? Well, then, drink." There is a cup on the railing by your hand. The water in it is cool, fresh, slightly sweet. It clears your head, and your emotions. You can feel it soothing and cooing as it goes down your throat.

"What are you seeking today? It is late for one with poor eyesight to be about alone on this path."

"But it never hurts to let yourself get lost, now and then, you know. Here you have a path of Wood to follow, so no worry about being lost. Remember, however, that if you get upset, or emotional in any way, the railing will become splintery, or even disappear. We can't have that, now, can we? No, you have to manage your emotions."

You take a breath to answer, but it beats you to it.

"No, no words, human. Just know your heart. Flow with life. That means let life flow through you, like the blood that is so necessary to your kind. And it means to accept what happens and deal with it as you go forward, let the emotions flow. If you dam them up, you will explode. You are not made to be a reservoir. It just does not work that way. Now, I am letting the rain come, because it must. But you need to seek home, you need its shelter."

You reach out and find the railing that follows the boardwalk, and you start following it. the drizzle has found a way down your back.

"Let it flow. It will wash you clean. Feel those splinters? Yes? That is because you are letting the emotions get the better of you."

J IS FOR JOVIAL AND JUDICIOUS.

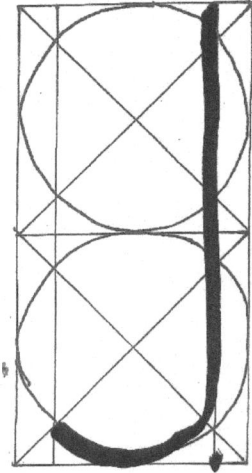

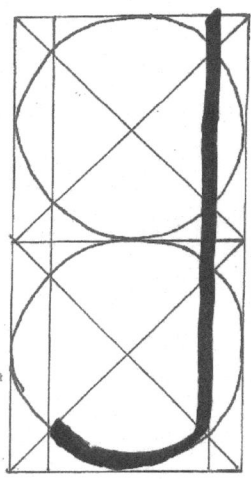

JOVIAL

Cheer up! Take a moment to laugh! Even when the world is falling apart, find some small corner of your being where a laugh can be lived. It releases tension, lets go of the stored energy in your tense muscles. It will feel good!

JUDICIOUS

Know your limits, and the limits of those around you. But also expect more, in increments that you can handle. Take a risk, every day, and do something unexpected. Do something you always felt you could not do, just a bit out of your comfort zone.

JONQUILS

Family: Amaryllus (Amaryllidaceae)
Genus: Narcissus jonquilla, Daffodil

Who does not love the daffodil in spring? With yellow that bursts out like a little sun, white that is pure as the snow, and orange determined to highlight the trumpet of the flower, what is not to like?

Often, Jonquil is applied to the dwarf flower varieties, but it makes little difference which term is used for which variety. They are all a joy to see in the spring.

The letter J is associated with the constellation of Leo, the lion. Its dates are July 23 to August 22. That puts it at the roaring center of the summer, which is appropriate. The Sun rules Leo, and it is a Fire sign.

The symbol for Leo is a curl that goes up and into a swoop toward the right. This is the mane of the lion, the arch of its back, and the twitching tail at the end.

Color choices can include the following.

Cancer's own color is yellow, with a complementary color of violet to bring out its vibrant nature.

Leo is a Fire sign, and the color for Fire is red, in all its intensity.

It is also ruled by the Sun, whose color is yellow.

The aim is to make the combination vibrant: experiment to find the best combination of colors for a Fiery Lion in the Sun of the African Savanna!

"You are perhaps wondering what this land is good for. It is so barren! Well, it has a lot to offer the enterprising traveler. There was no detail when you first stepped on this path. Did you see anything? No. No one ever does."

J does a strange twisting movement which allows it to sit, although it is hard to describe that with the many parts of its outfit.

"Once you paid attention to the information your eyes were gathering, you began to see the details of this land. Yes? You were paying attention. You spent time looking for choices. Oh! You did indeed! Many choices, all wrapped into one. Go on or turn back? And what did you do?"

J pauses to look attentively at you. What is it looking for? Well, you cannot know, so you simply wait for more information.

"Information: you paid attention to what you know about hot and dry, about desert, and about not seeing any water. You looked at the plants in the dips, the chances of rain in the sky all the signals of the environment. You gathered that information quickly, but you did gather it."

J shifts a little to be more comfortable. "Evaluation: you matched past knowledge against the evidence you gathered about the environment. You reduced the options to two: continue on or go back. You missed the third, which was to stand still. By default, that choice was dismissed."

The voice is becoming more jovial, enjoying the process of evaluating the situation. "Decision: you based your choice on the accomplishment of your goal to finish the path, and to meet me on the way. You chose to meet me. That is why you found me so quickly after making the choice to continue on your way. Very rational, very moral, very goal-driven."

K IS FOR KINDNESS AND KNOWLEDGE.

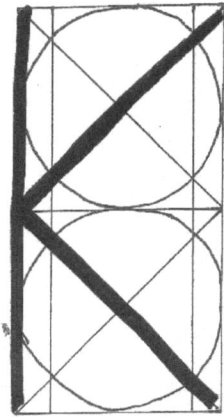

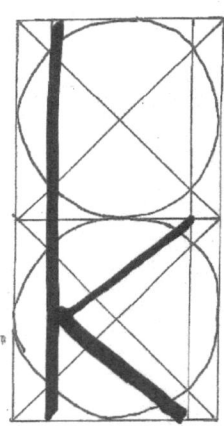

KINDNESS

It will never hurt you to be kind. It feels good. It makes friends. It opens your heart. So, why are you not kind? Take the time to look for things you can do to help others, to help yourself. Then feel good for doing it.

KNOWLEDGE

Thought is best when based in fact. At its root, fact and reality keep knowledge real. But sometimes you have to take a chance, shoot the arrow of your mind into the wide blue sky so you can expand your knowledge to the next level of knowing.

KING DEVIL

Family: Daisy (Compositae)

Genus: Hieracium pratense

This is a member of the Hawkweek group, with tall stalks of flowers in yellows and oranges. This particular one is hardy in fields and by the roadside. It has lots of hairs on it, and grows up to about three feet.

You will see this flower from spring to late summer. Once you find it, you will see it all the time. Until then, it may be a struggle to locate one.

The letter K is associated with Sagittarius, the Arrow. Its dates are November 23 to December 21. Somehow, that is appropriate: the speed of an arrow matches the speed with which events travel between Thanksgiving and New Year!

The symbol for Sagittarius is an arrow. The point is aimed outward, and the bottom has a feather to steady th flight. This combines with the letter K because the letter looks like the arrow hit it and pushed the middle of the right side into the stem on the left!

Color choices are as follows.

The color for Sagittarius is blue, with a complementary color of orange.

Sagittarius is a Fire sign, so red can be used.

It is also ruled by Jupiter, whose color is blue. This matches the constellation's own color of blue.

"You were thinking about your goals on that walk, weren't you? Yes, many people come this way, and most of them say that is what the savannah draws out of them. Do you have a clear fix on those goals? Can you tell them clearly and quickly? You really should get them straight. But here is another thought. Go a little further. Check what your values are. Make sure each of your goals is on a par with your values. And of course, make sure that you have goals to help you develop your values, too."

In the long silence that follows, you begin the process suggested. You notice that several goals go directly against your values. That makes no sense! Why would you pursue goals that break your values? Huh. Guess there is some thinking and adjusting that will have to be done.

"Every few years, check your values. They may change. It won't be by much, but it could conflict with your goals." K goes silent again, apparently thinking about the subject.

L IS FOR LOVING AND LIVELINESS.

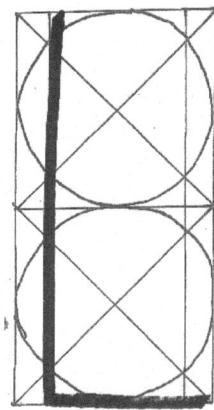

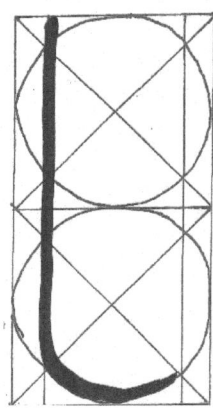

LOVING

Everything is better with love. Open your heart and let the love in. Open your heart and let the love out. Share it with everyone. Share it with everything. And then, express it so everyone knows they are loved!

LIVELINESS

Wake up! Move! Jump up and down, wiggle your backside, tap your toes! Don't just sit there, DO something! Look lively now, you have a life to live! What are you waiting for?

LILY

Family: Lily (Liliaceae)

Genus: artistic rendition

Here is another variation on a plant: the leaves are not quite right, so it is not a specific genus. But lilies come in all kinds of colors, including spotted tiger lilies, all-white Easter lilies, and orange day lilies. So, let your imagination run wild on the colors! Here is your chance to use the colors you never would use in making this or that specific flower!

The letter L is associated with Libra, the scales. Its dates are September 24 to October 23. This is the time when autumn begins, and school starts up again. It is an Air sign, and is ruled by Venus.

The symbol for libra has a flat line for the pan in which something is placed so it can be measured on the scale. The top has an arch that rests on an upright (which is not part of the symbol).

Colors that can be used include the following.

Libra's color is green, and the complementary color is red.

As an Air sign, yellow can be used.

The ruling planet is Venus, whose color is green.

Use this letter to experiment with the various kinds of green that you will find in your set of paint, markers, pencils or crayons.

L gracefully glides over the ground, first leaning forward, then backward, with eyes set high at the end of the upper serif. When it reaches the pool, it continues toward you, the bottom leg hidden under water.

L tips its head down to look into your eyes. "Like this place?" You nod yes. "Least you have good taste."

L comes out of the water an turns to face the ppool with you. After a moment, L begins a conversation. "You balanced?" Thinking back on the way you got here, you know that you are. "Good. It's important. Keep a good balance in your life. When were you out in nature last? Oh, I can sense it has been quite a while. At least get a houseplant. That will help. Want you to think on something."

L is silent for a bit, in spite of that statement. Then, lifting up a twig with an ant on it, L continues.

"Little ant! Yes, part of nature. Knows a thing or two. Hard worker. Keeps faith with the rest of the colony." L examines the ant in great detail. Then the twig and ant are tossed into the water near the water strider. "There you go, little ant! End your life." The water strider promptly takes the ant and eats it. This is not what you expected.

"Now, little ant, you are a water strider! Think of that! What a transformation!" L is pleased with the transformation. "You weren't expecting that, were you? Well, maybe the ant wasn't either. But really, if you think about it, life is a balance between predator and prey, living and dying. Everything has to eat. Fact of life. No sentiment about it. Let's go up to the falls."

M IS FOR MEMORY AND MESSAGES.

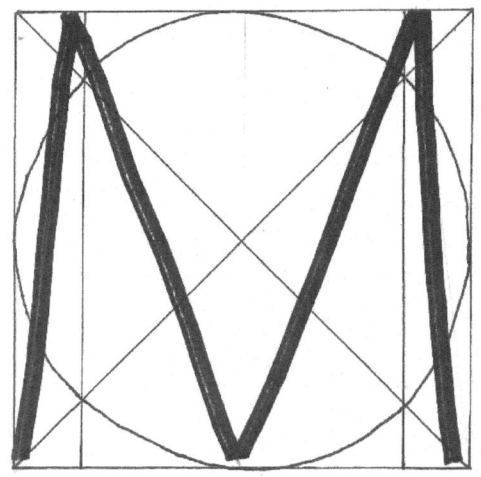

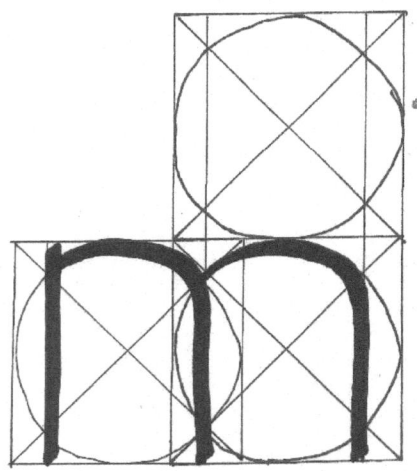

MEMORY

Remember when you were happy? Remember when the sky shone with sunshine and the rain only came when the garden needed it? Remember when you were able to do what you wanted? Keep that memory alive! It belongs to you, and stays with you as long as you remember you have it.

MESSAGES

Oh! The mail is here! Letters from friends who are far away will fill the morning with happy messages from afar! Check that post on the internet—yes! There is a message from around the world! Friends and acquaintances are speaking!

MULBERRY

Family: Fig (Moraceae)
Genus: Morus nigra

Birds love Mulberry. And the seeds are happy to pass through their digestive system! The Mulberry will volunteer: if you don't want it, root it up before it gets settled in.

The male Mulberry makes a tremendous amount of pollen, which is a problem if you have asthma, but the female will absorb the pollen of any plant around it. That makes it nearly pollen-free, and good for asthma!

The berry is edible, and is shaped a lot like the blackberries. Silk worms are fed mulberry leaves, and the bark has been used to make paper.

Then again, children sing "ring around the mulberry bush" as they do a circle dance. So there are many uses for this bush-tree.

The letter M is associated with Virgo, the virgin, and is in charge of the dates from August 23 to September 23. It is an Earth sign that is ruled by Mercury.

The symbol for Virgo is a discrete M; the end of the letter on the right curves back, like a virgin demurely crossing her legs. Remember that the symbols were developed a very, very long time ago, when such things were thought of in a completely different way.

Color choices can include any of the following suggestions.

The color for Virgo is yellow-green, so its complementary color is red-violet. That is sometimes called magenta.

The color for Mercury, the ruling planet of this sign, is orange.

The color for the element of Earth is different in different traditions. Generally, black can be used, because it is the color of rich and fertile earth. Or, brown for soil, or green for growing things can be used. If you use brown, look for a rich brown, perhaps with a hint of red or orange in it.

Overhead there are bats darting as they chase after bugs, especially mosquitoes. Their high-pitched voices are barely audible, but their services are appreciated. A gentle breeze moves the scented air around the field, making gentle rustling sounds in the grass. Overhead, the Milky Way spreads its brilliance from horizon to horizon.

"It is all a matter of perspective. First you are wandering about aimlessly in life, unable to focus on anything. Then you become so overwhelmed that you are frozen and unable to move in any direction at all. What you need is perspective. That is what resolves the opposite ends of that spectrum."

M gestures to the whole sky with its eyes. "All of this, all this wonderful expanse, all the myriad stars, they are all just one part of the world we live in. It is all useless, though, when we fail to take the time to look, to pay attention. You have to grab experiences by the shoulder and shake it until the right fruit falls out. Oh, nuts. That didn't come out right at all. But perhaps you see what I am getting at anyway? Yes? Good. I have run out of pictures to describe. I do much better with the space pictures, to be honest. Like all astronomers, I look at the part of the sky that is needed for the current survey, and never seem to have time to look at the beauty. Well, balance and perspective are the solution. That is why I come out here to this smaller, amateur observatory. This sky, like it is tonight, reminds me why I love astronomy so much."

"Now and again, you have to go back to what drives you. Yes, duty is important, doing what we have contracted to do, and do it well. And of course, all sorts of things go into keeping our health on line. Yes, me too. I have to be careful of my diet. I am getting rather rounded in the middle, don't you think? But the real thing is to get to the substance of what drives us."

N IS FOR NEGOTIATION AND NERVOUSNESS.

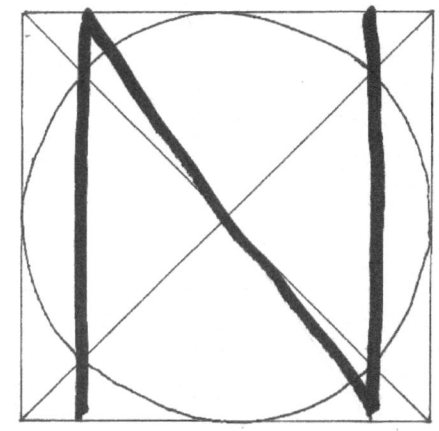

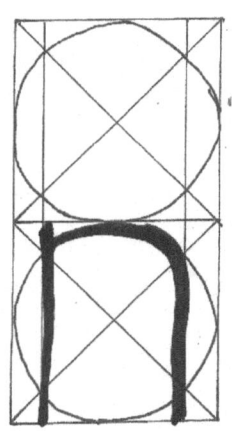

NEGOTIATION

Working with others, we always have to negotiate. There is a common ground in the issue, we just have to communicate back and forth until we can find it. And then, both sides of the situation can agree to the outcome.

NERVOUSNESS

How often we are nervous about the outcome of an important meeting! Butterflies fill the belly; nerves are set on edge. In the end, the answer is either yes or no. Until the answer is known, wit is better to wait patiently for the outcome. Too bad the nerves don't ever seem to learn that!

NELUMBO

Family: Water-lily (Nymphaeaceae)

Genus: Nelumbo lutea, American Lotus

Here is a real beauty! This yellow water lily eases the changes from summer into winter with its leaves cupped above the water. It likes stagnant water, and is a real surprise whenever it is seen.

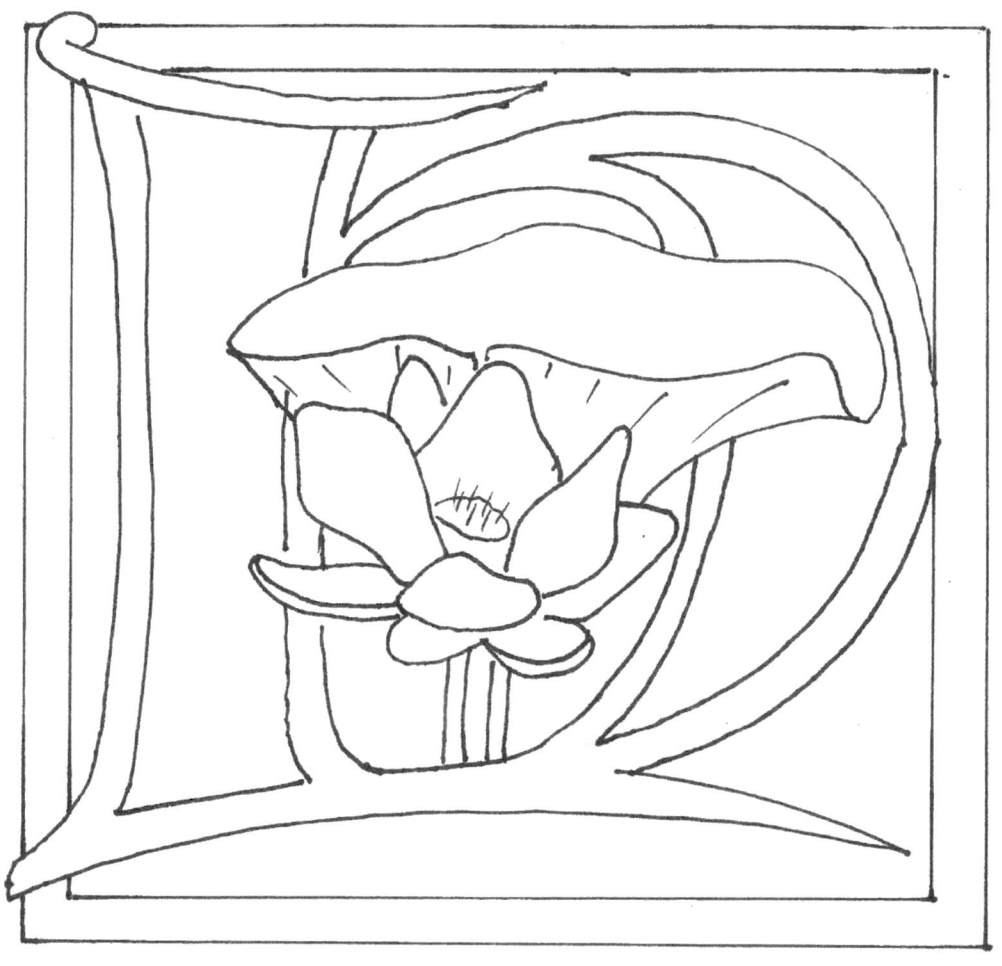

The letter N is associated with the planet Mercury, the planet of tricksters, guides of the dead, scholars, merchants, and travel in general. It covers a lot of territory!

The symbol for Mercury is complex. Some like to call it the little man with horns. A better way to see it is to break it into parts. The horns are the crescent Moon. The circle is the Sun. The cross at the bottom is the horizontal female and the vertical male, in balance. Sun and Moon, male and female, perfect balance. This is appropriate, since Mercury is generally a figure that is not very easily given a gender.

Color choices can include any of the following.

The color for Mercury itself is orange, with a complementary color of blue.

The element for Mercury is Water, so again blue can be used.

Remember, this design is planned to vibrate, so sharp orange and blue are appropriate. However, we have already talked about doing other things with the color combinations. Here is a perfect time to experiment!

"Well, well, well, what have we here? You a Traveler to the land of the dead? Well, here are the books, all nice and dead. Or you need me to lead you into death? I can do that, don't like to, though. No? Well, what then?"

It pauses, then makes a final guess. "Ah! You are on a journey of discovery! You wanted to meet me! Oh! What fun! Well, howdy-do! Come, sit. We shall chat for a bit!"

"Well. So. I have some knowledge about a lot of things, and as you see, I have access to a lot more than I hold in my own brain. Yes, I have a brain. May not look like yours, but I asure you it is there."

Looking around, you are impressed by the magnitude of the knowledge contained in the library. "No question goes unanswered. Problem is, the answer often is not what you want it to be. That can be problematic. Downright disappointing. But it is what it is. Logic rules here. Did you notice the nice, neat labels for everything as you came in? Yes! Worked for centuries to get that sorted out."

"So. here's the thing. This whole library is useless if you don't know what you are trying to find out. But give me a question, zip-zap, quick as that, I can find the right book or whatever to guide you to the right answer. But of course, not all books tell truth. That you have to figure out for yourself. Ha-ha-ha! That is the beauty of books! Tell you truth and lies, all mixed together. Kind of makes you think! That is the whole trick, of course. You have to think."

"I am rambling again. Well, this is a library. Best information sometimes is the random piece that is not looked for.

O IS FOR ORGANIZATION AND OBSESSION.

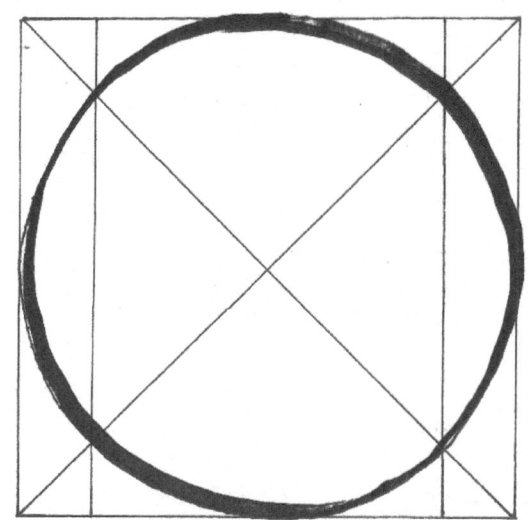

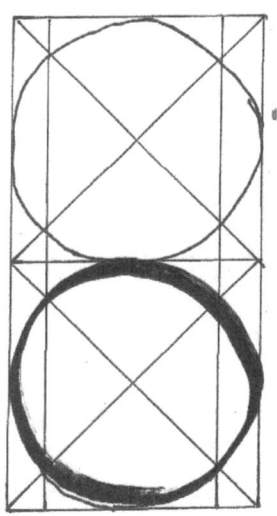

ORGANIZATION

First, second, third: there is an order that can fix the chaos. Trouble is, we get so wrapped up in things that we forget to check the organization we are trying to find. Take a step back and look at things again. Look for the order that will help make things better.

OBSESSION

Nothing gets in the way of the thought or feeling that is filling your head and heart. You simply will not let it go. Well, is it worth the effort? Is it what you really want? If so, maybe the obsession can help you through the delays in getting what you are aiming for.

ORANGE BLOSSOMS

Family: Hydrangea (Hydrangacea)

Genus: Philadelphus coronaries, Mock Orange Blossom

Ahh! The gentle scent of spring! This bush is a perfect addition to any landscape, giving a gentle but distinct reminder of the orange orchards of the south. They grow in the north, allowing those who have never experiences an orchard of orange trees to enjoy the delicious aroma of this beautiful bush.

The flowers are purest white, with a cheery yellow center. And they flower prolifically, making each branch a real treasure.

For those near orange orchards, the breeze can also pick up the incredible scent and carry it across fields to captivate and entrance any who encounter it. Once you have experienced this, you will be able to recall the beauty by closing your eyes, taking a deep breath and remembering the sunshine and aroma on the air.

Both scents are entrancing, depending on where you live.

The letter O is associated with the element Fire. Its zesty nature adds spice and energy to our lives, and represents both the destruction of a fire, and the constructive energy to build things.

The symbol for Fire is a triangle pointing upward. All flames tend to point upward, and burn through nearly everything.

The color choices for Fire include a wide selection of colors, all centered around the color red.

It is hard to think of green as part of fire, but that is the complementary color for Fire's red.

The flame can be seen as being anything from red to yellow-orange. That range includes:

Red

Red-orange

Orange

Yellow-orange

The combinations work out better if the colors used are pure, not mixed. So, burgundy (dark red) is less likely to suggest fire, and pale orange (peach) is too gentle for fire.

As you lean forward toward the campfire, the O speaks. "Whoa there! You can burn inside, but I can't answer for that wet body of yours if you come too close. Back up a bit. OK. Now lets talk a bit."

"This is me when I am let loose. But most of the time you are meeting me, it will be as some other form of energy. Whoa! Look at that!" O has turned around to watch the bonfire, as the logs fall in on the fire, releasing a storm of red sparks to fly high into the sky in a show of defiance against the destruction taking place in the fire.

"You won't ever tame me, you know. But maybe we can work together with the energies you already have in you. That would be fun! Just think of all the wonderful things we can do!"

Images of projects that wait to be done, games to be played, trips to take, work to be accomplished, all flash before your mind's eye. It is bewildering, confusing, and provocative. Everything to be done all at once—but you know that will not work. Just as you are about to say so, the O has more to say.

"Up to you. Do it all. I suggest one thing at a time, but, hey, it's your life. Keep at it. When you run out of energy, blow on the embers to get the flame back. Stoke your fire so the rain doesn't put it out. I will give you a magical chant to get all the work done. Want to hear it? Here it is."

There is a pause, then the words ring out, filling the entire campsite. They echo in your ears. "MORE WOOD!"

"Now go on, get out of here. You sat ong enough. Go! Get something done! Doesn't matter what, you know, just do it. keep on doing. Always active! Do! Do! Do!"

P IS FOR PRUDENCE AND PATIENCE.

PRUDENCE

Plan ahead, be sure you are as ready for the future as you can be. But don't get carried away by conspiracy theories and doomsday pronouncements. None of them have come true yet! Still, some reasonable preparation for the future will help.

PATIENCE

It takes time to get what is worth getting. All the beginning steps are needed before any mastery can be achieved. Relax, take it one step at a time, in some reasonable order, and you will get to the goals you have set.

PINKS

Family: Gentian (Gentianaceae)

Genus: Sabatia angularis, Rose-Pink

Small, scarce, and gemlike when found: that is the Rose-Pink. But when you find it, you will see that it has five petals, not four.

They are, indeed, pink.

While you may find them on the edge of a field, watch your feet. The ground will be quite moist or wet. And don't bother to look in a garden. It is all stem, and gardeners like plants that are fuller than this.

Pinks show up as a surprise! Hunting for them is hard, so it is best to enjoy your summer hike, and be open to the chance encounter with this short beauty.

The letter P is associated with Aquarius, the water bearer. It is an Air sign, ruled by Saturn. Its dates are January 20 to February 19.

The symbol for Aquarius is flowing water that turns into air. The sign is actually not a water sign: which surprises some. No: it is the process of pouring the water that is the focus. P was chosen to represent this, but showing the pot (loop of the P) with the water (stem) flowing out, through the air, toward the ground.

The colors that are assigned to this letter include the following.

Aquarius is given violet, or purple. The complementary color is yellow.

As an Air sign, the color of Air is yellow.

Saturn is the ruling planet, and its color is red-violet, or magenta, and can be shown with bright rose.

Vibrations radiate into your feet: thump-thump, a heavy tread behind you. Turning, you see a huge elephant coming down the path, with others behind her. Prudence makes you move to the shelter of the nearest strong tree. The stately pace and vocal exchanges of the great beasts are impressive as they pass. One small elephant, no higher than four feet, stops to extend its trunk to you, sniffing you out. Its sibling nudges it forward, and they all pass by.

A few sun rays that you can see are nearly horizontal now. There is not much time left to find shelter. Just as you begin to truly worry, a large P steps out on the path in front of you.

"What are you waiting for? Come on! Come on! Time to get inside the village!"

As the sun hits the horizon, the world's light goes out there is no dusk here: the sun is up and bright, or down and dark.

"You have explored your inner sense of security and safety, haven't you? Yes, I see it in your eyes. Important issue. Can't live without it. Security, I mean. It is the key to the safety that overcomes fear and lets you get things done. But fear is needed too, isn't it? You stepped aside for the elephants; I saw you. Yes. That was wise of you. No sense inviting harm when none is intended."

Q IS FOR QUALITY AND QUANTITY.

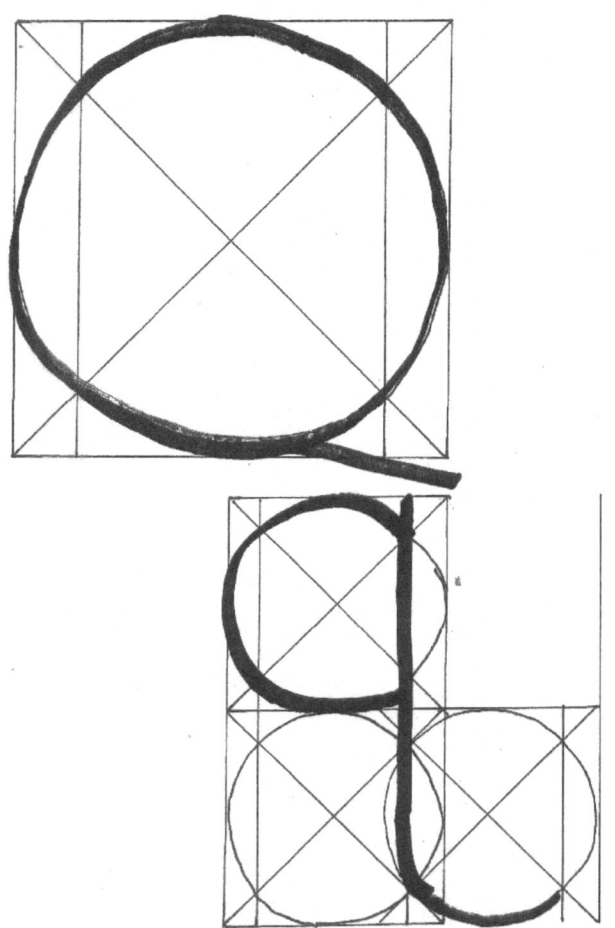

QUALITY

If you want something to last, it is best to invest in quality. Slipshod and half baked are not long-term investment goals. Wait until you can afford the time and energy to get the best, and then it will last for a lifetime.

QUANTITY

Some situations call for repetition and numbers to overcome the resistance to progress in life. So, sometimes invest in quantity. Some part of that large number will survive the test of time.

QUEEN ANN'S LACE

Family: Parsley (Umbelliferae)

Genus: Daucus carota

If you worry about confusion with Poison Hemlock (that did in Socrates), look for the purple cross in the center of the flower: small, but its presence helps identify the plant. The truth is, once you know the Wild Carrot, you will never confuse it with Hemlock. But for the beginner, the confusion is real, so be careful.

Watch the flowers as they age: when pollinated, they turn into Bird's Nests by curling the edges of the flower in on itself and turning brown. The seeds are a wonderful flavoring in stew, but be sure to use them in a gauze pouch: they are not easy to chew or digest. The root is a white, woody carrot, also good in cooking. But only use it as flavoring: it is really woody and tough!

This is a transplanted weed from Europe that is beautiful and graceful. The hardy plant belies the delicate foliage and flower. If you plant it, expect flowers in the second year. And remember, it likes fields, dry places, and junk soil.

The letter Q is associated with the planet Earth. This is different than the element Earth, which is represented by the letter U. This is our home, planet of our birth.

The symbol for planet Earth is a circle with an X in it. We say, 'X marks the spot', which refers to our home, where we live. The circle is the planet, or the cycle of life on our planet.

The colors have been changing over time, but here are some suggestions.

In home décor, the Earth colors are ochre, avocado, and rust.

Another system gives: citrine, olive, russet, and black.

NASA has shown us a planet that is blue, white, green and tan.

Fertile ground is black, or rich brown (with a tint of red or orange).

Rock is grey, black, or any number of other colors, depending on the bedrock where you grew up.

Life is best represented by the lush green of plant life.

There are, as you can see, many options for the colors of planet Earth. Perhaps NASA is right: we are a big, blue marble in space. But don't forget the green growth of life, and the white of the clouds.

139

Its sad eyes finally notice you, and it looks up into your eyes.

"Have you seen my U anywhere about here?"

It continues to look for an answer, and as you are about to speak, Q suddenly lights up, smiling brightly.

"You! I knew I would find U! Thank goodness! I thought you had gone forever." It has clearly confused 'y-o-u' with 'U'.

Q is leaping with joy. Well, leaping is a general word. It leans on the extended leg and uses it as a spring to push its round body off the ground, then repeats again when it comes down. Its smile is bright with joy. As Q settles a bit, the joy remains, but the dancing stops.

"I am so useless without U. I depend so completely on it. Thank you for bringing U to visit! Yes, you have it in you. It is at your feet; I can see it. Right where you put it before you came here. Oh! What a relief! And now, with your U and my Q, we can chat for a bit!"

"You know, I have heard some folks say that I should be more grounded. I guess that is what U does for me. We are so closely related, and U can just make me focus and sound like I know what I am doing."

R IS FOR RESPONSIBILITY AND RULERSHIP.

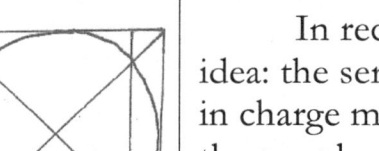

RESPONSIBILITY

If it is your job, do it, and do it well. If it is your job, the do it without putting it onto someone else. No passing the buck, no dilly-dallying. Just pick up the work and get it done as well as you are able to do it.

RULERSHIP

In recent times, we have developed an idea: the servant leader. This means that being in charge means that you have responsibility to the people you lead. What is often forgotten is that the first rulership we each must take up is over our own selves and our own lives. That is the most important responsibility we each carry through life.

RASPBERRIES

Family: Rose (Rosacea)

Genus: Rubus odoratus

All raspberries are attractive to birds, and that shows in the spread of the bush! It is a five-petal bush that spreads like all its relatives, and has leaves that will remind you of a maple tree.

The berries are a natural trail mix: they are best eaten one or two at a time when found. You will not want to get into the middle of the bush: it is prickly. Just enjoy a few of the berries when you see them.

The letter R is associated with Capricorn, the sea goat. This is a Zodiac sign ruled by Saturn, and it is an Earth sign. Its dates are December 22 to January 19. While the Sun is at its weakest (Northern Hemisphere), this is the season when most cultures celebrate their festivals of light.

The symbol of Capricorn is a bit odd, as is the creature it represents. With the front end of a goat (on the left) and the tail of a fish (right side), there is a combination of Earth and Water. Yet, the sign is an Earth sign, not a Water sign. So, the balance of power goes to the head, the goat's front end.

Colors for Capricorn include blue-violet, with its compliment of yellow-orange.

The color for Saturn is red-violet, or magenta.

The color for the element Earth is black, brown, or dark green.

While you consider the answer to that question, R moves about again. "You know, there is a balance needed here. You are so passive; I think I finally have found a way to describe ennui! You are overcome by it. No movement, just passively resting. Now, outside, there is complete chaos. Movement all over the place, without purpose, just random. You are just like the snowflakes out there. They are just blown about too, just like you were getting here. But you want to make a difference in your life, to evolve in some small way. That is why you are here. So, you have to put the chaos and the ennui together, to mix them up, and then you will have a balanced energy to evolve with. It is all up to you. It is a balance, but you have to want the balance to work, and you have to continue to keep it balanced."

"The tea tastes refreshing, just as it is, without any cream or sugar. It is complete. It is fresh, made with fresh water and fresh (dried, but only three months old) leaves. Together they refresh. If you put something more in, the balance would be disturbed. If you use stale tea, the balance would be disturbed. It's all about the balance! Ah! The tea is refreshing, isn't it?"

The wood crackles with the fire's heat. The air is filled with a warm scent of pine needles that reminds you of festive winter holidays and family gatherings. The light in the room is warm and inviting, and you feel peace in the moment. Beyond the door, the gale winds blow and howl, but do not touch you, in here, by the fire.

S IS FOR STRENGTH AND SEVERITY.

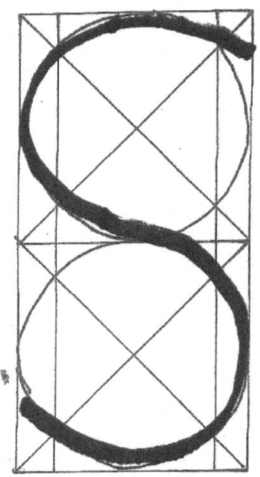

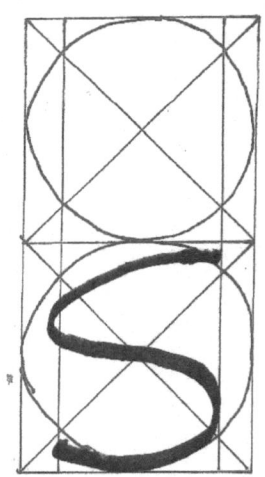

STRENGTH

It is easy to think that strength means physical ability. It actually goes into every part of life: strength in handling emotions; strength in holding to our beliefs; strength in facing the universe of possibilities that opens before us when we are striving to be the best person we are capable of in life.

SEVERITY

Hard things are hard. They are unavoidable, they force hard decisions, they cannot be avoided. Muster up the strength to face the hard facts and deal with them in the best way you can. One step at a time will get you to the other side.

SAGITTARIA

Family: Arrowhead (Alismataceae)

Genus: Sagittaria latifolia, Broad-leaved Arrowhead

Best seen in still ponds, the leaf of this plant will catch your eye: there is no question it is an Arrow head, with its point toward the sky and two tails holding it back toward the water!

The flower is interesting: there are not a lot of flowers with just three petals, and nearly none that bloom in the summer.

For the botanist, there are a lot of species related to this plant. They are nearly the same, with slight variations. For our purposes, this is a generally common plant along the edges of ponds. We leave the fine tuning to those who want to study the genus.

The letter S is associated with Scorpio, the scorpion. This is the Zodiac sign that rules from October 24 to November 22. It is a Water sign ruled by Mars. Some say by Pluto, but that is a planet that needs a telescope to see, and is therefore not one of the traditional seven planets.

The symbol for Scorpio is an M with a stinger: the stinger is the most noticeable characteristic of the scorpion.

The color choices for Scorpio includes the following.

Scorpio is blue-green, and its complement red-orange.

Water is blue, in all its tints, shades and hues.

Mars is the red planet: its color is red, usually very bright and clean. Avoid burgundy and crimson.

"Ever wonder what it would be like to wander among the stars? No, I mean really wander, physically, like when you walk through the woods, no direct purpose, just to wonder at the beauty."

There is a long pause. "Some think the universe is moribund. Dead. Nothing moving or changing. Others think all the astronomical movement is just frenetic, aimless motion. Personally, I think of it as lively, a balance of static and active processes. I like lively yes, that is a good word for it."

S looks at you. "What are you going to o next? I mean, really, you are just sitting here like there is no tomorrow. What are you doing tomorrow?"

You open your mouth to answer, but S beats you to it. "No matter. You don't have to tell me. Oh, look, the fire is going out. MORE WOOD!" From the soft voice to a lout call, the sudden change in volume is startling. After tending to the fire for a bit, you sit back and relax again.

"The key, of course, is to take full responsibility for whatever project you undertake. If you don't, all the results will be weak and useless. So, take responsibility for the process and the results will look after themselves. But on the other hand, don't overdo the control or you will burn out from the demands of the project. I get to slither between the two extremes, you don't. I don't envy you that. You have to stand there and be responsible, but not too much, not too little. Must be very tiring. Don't think I could do it."

T IS FOR TRUST AND thinking

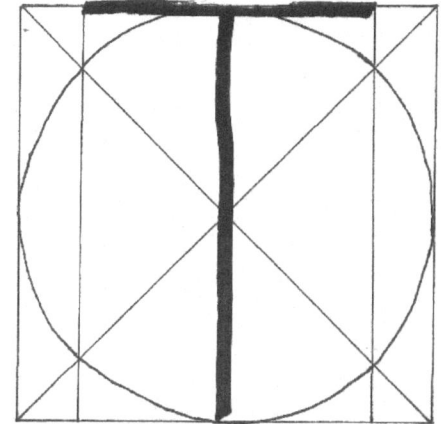

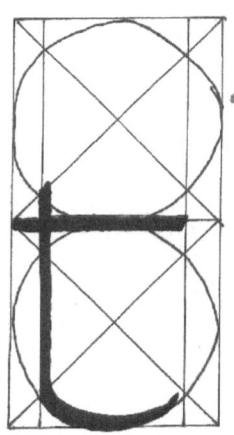

TRUST

When you believe in someone, they are better able to live up to your trust. That goes for trusting yourself, too! Know your own mind, and trust your own wisdom. It will get you farther than you might imagine.

THINKING

Stop. Just stop and look. Consider, evaluate, ponder. Work it through. You can come up with better courses of action if you think it over and allow new ideas to pop up.

TREES

Family: Beech (Fagaceae)
Genus: Quercus alba, White Oak

Ahh! Trees! What a delightfully broad category! There are so many kinds, we have to be content with just one.

The arbitrary choice here is the Oak. Even with that narrowing of focus, there are about 450 choices.

The fruit of the oak tree is an acorn. In World War II, the English used the acorn to make flour for baking, because they had little or no wheat. The problem is that the acorn can be bitter. This requires soaking the acorn to let the bitterness dissolve out. Then you have to grind it. This process makes acorn flour a survival food: good to eat if you really need it, but a lot of bother to do acceptably.

Oak gives strong wood for furniture, and grows large for shade. It often was planted outside the blacksmith's forge, which makes it the tree in the center of the village.

Oak is said to be hit by lightning more often than other trees. So it is associated with thunder gods like Thor.

The letter T is associated with Jupiter, the gas giant that is far out in the solar system. It is a Water planet. Jupiter rules the heavens, bestowing gifts and striking with lightning. In myth, Jupiter is the sky-god, although we tend to think more in terms of the emperor or CEO of a corporation.

The symbol of Jupiter is a great cross of the male/vertical and female/horizontal, combined with the crescent Moon.

The color of Jupiter is blue, with a complementary color of orange.

All the tints, shades, and hues of blue are used in representing this planet.

"This is the most important window. It is all about leadership, and how to lead in the best way you can. You see, there is the leader," as the T points to a figure in a deep blue cape. The figure is bending over a hoe that he is using to weed a small vegetable plot. Nearby is a small hut, with a figure laying just inside the door. "The true leader is happy to help out those he leads when they need an extra hand. See, he is smiling, not scolding, and he has already almost completed the job."

This is an interesting idea, and you take it in. the leader is happy to do whatever is needed, even manual labor and jobs he is not normally expected to do. You notice that his crown is set to the side, on the ground. How appropriate!

"And over here," says T, moving to the first window on the opposite side of the room, "is the most important window. It shows the joy of groups of people coming together to work on a common task." On this window, you see a group of men, women and children gathered for a meal at a table under a broad tree. Everyone is happy and smiling, and nearby a few are playing instruments and dancing. Everyone seems to be in a jovial mood.

T now moves to the other window on the same wall. "Here we have the most important window. See how the leader is taking the shackles off the worker? She is offering forgiveness and mercy to one of the villagers. Notice that she is not washing away the dirt on the prisoner's face or hands. Mercy has memory too, not just forgiveness. You have to remember what was done, but you have to help the person move on too." You examine the image, and notice that there are indications that the leader will give the prisoner aid in more tangible form to help make a fresh start.

U IS FOR URGENT AND UNCONSCIOUS.

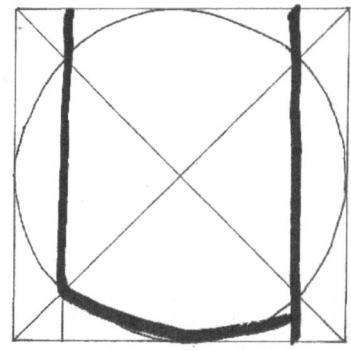

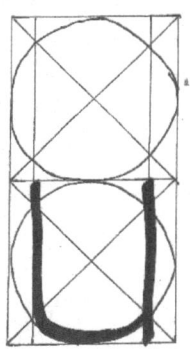

URGENT

Quick! Now, before it is too late! Hurry up! No time to waste. If you don't do it now, when can it ever be done again? No slacking now. Immediate attention is needed!

UNCONSCIOUS

Hidden, subtle, driving but not known: the unconscious thought will push and prod until you get it up out of the basement and into the light where you can look it over and figure it out.

UVULARIA

Family: Lily (Liliaceae)

Genus: Uvularia grandiflora, Large-flowered Bellwort

Why is it that so many beautiful flowers have such questionable names?

Walking through the woods in spring, you may happen upon this little yellow flower. It likes shade, especially maple forests. You may happen upon a patch of these strange flowers.

The flower itself hangs like a limp rag. It is completely facing downward, with the entire stem drooped. And that stem does something else strange: it seems to pierce the leaves! The stem passes through the base of the leaf, which clasps around it completely.

So, listen for the spring birds when you look for this one. They will not lead you to it, but will form a soundtrack behind the experience.

The letter U is associated with the element Earth, a way of understanding the rest of the elements touching ground, remaining tied to reality and not flying off. It can be like having rocks in your head, or like planting your feet in the ground.

The symbol for element Earth is a triangle pointing down, with a line across it. the triangle lets us know that this element is beneath our feet, and the line tells us it is filled and solid.

The colors for the element Earth include dark green, green, sometimes brown like the rich dirt of planet Earth.

The complement of dark green is burgundy, a form of dark red.

The complement of brown is navy blue, since brown is a form of dark orange.

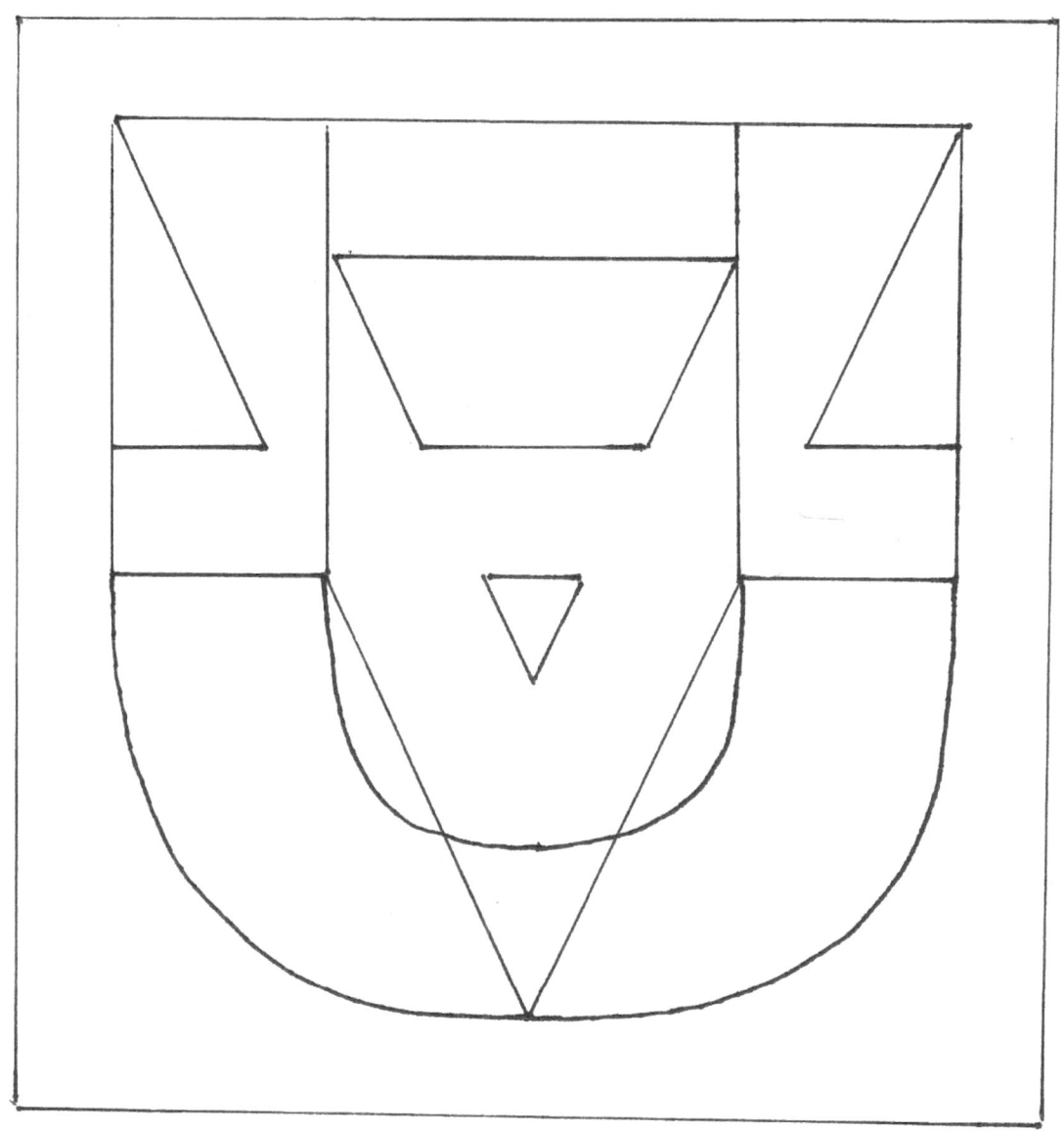

"Well! Took you long enough to get here! Been waiting all evening for you. Glad to meet you."

"I suppose you want to have a long chat over some warm beverage? Well, I don't do fire. Have to ask O for that. Me, all I want is to get things rooted and growing. Now, a leaf, fallen by itself, that I can offer you to chew. Here, try this one…"

U leans its head down to the ground and nudges a fallen leaf toward you. "Go ahead. Chew on it for a while. No need to fear. It will help you hear the speech of those plants around here. Wonderful skill to have. Unless they are upset. Then it is just chaos. All yammering at the same time. Where are you going?"

As you begin to answer U interrupts. "You are going to U, aren't you? Hmph. Well, here you are. You need to get to know U, which is to say, YOU. Go home with that and play with it for a while. It will make more sense later."

U moves closer and gestures to you that you should bend over. It seems there is a secret to be given to you.

"Turn around. No, not now. When I finish. Turn around, and go back another way. Don't go the same way you came. What would be the point in that? It's a U-turn, certainly, but not to redo the past. Go parallel to the path you came by. Do you understand? No? Well, let the Guardian of Earth help you out if you don't know what to do."

U moves back a bit, looks you over, then mumbles and begins to wander off. Turning just the head, U says, as if over the shoulder, "have to go change into more comfortable garb. It is late. Time for bed. Well, for sleep. Or at least for being silent for a bit. Don't disturb the animals too much. I want a quiet evening, no nonsense. Nice meeting you." U disappears into the shrubbery.

V IS FOR VIBRANCY AND VIRILITY.

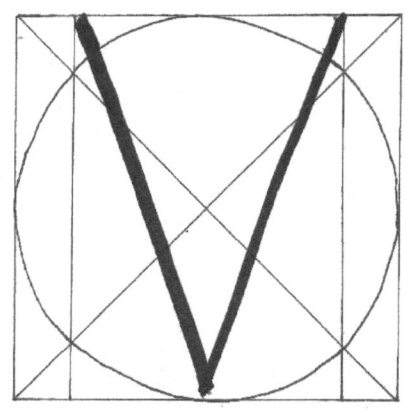

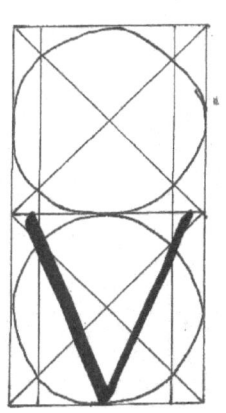

VIBRANCY

There is an excitement buried in this word. It is lively, ready to explode with life and possibility. Give in to it if you want to enliven your life.

VIRILITY

The force of strength can push matters forward with speed and distance. Be sure that the results are what you want, and be sure you know what is likely to happen before you chance a runaway process.

VIOLET

Family: Violet (Violaceae)

Genus: Viola papilionacea, Common Violet

This little spring beauty is no shrinking violet! If it likes the corner of your garden where you put it, you will be surprised at the dense growth of dark leaves and even darker flowers it will put up. Even the stems of the leaves will be violet colored!

The books all say they like a bit of shade. But gardeners will tell you that what they really want is to be remembered when you water the garden. The leaves all fall over when that happens, as if they are wilted. Actually, this exposes the roots so they can get all the water you give them.

The leaves are edible. But be careful: they are a laxative! Small violet candies are a delight, and bring little old ladies with their tea service to mind.

The scent is memorable, but does not travel very far from the plant. Distinctive is not the same as pervasive!

The letter V is associated with Aries, the ram. It is the Zodiac sign for the month starting on March 30 and goes to April 21. It is a Fire sign ruled by Mars.

The symbol for Aries is the ram's horns. This is very compatible with the V shape.

The color choices for Aries and for V are actually somewhat limited.

Aries color is red, with a complementary color of green.

Fire is red.

Mars is red.

This is a lot of red. Using tints and shades is hard, since both tend to be weaker colors than the pure red. But if you look at your paint, pencil, marker or crayon, you will see that there are several choices that are various types of red. Be creative, stretch your understanding of the color, and find your own solution!

"You are made of stern stuff. Few get to meet me this far up." V is dancing around, prancing on its tip as if it were on a spring. It makes you think of the way the Ram leapt from unseen outcrop to shelf and back again.

"This is the highest you can go. I see you have no air tank, so you will not be able to breathe any higher up. That is ok. Here I am, so you do not need to ascend any further." There is no doubt in V's mind that it is important enough to be the object of a difficult journey: it is more an acceptance of a role than it is a matter of ego.

A gust of wind catches you and pushes you to the ground. You are on hands and knees and facing the very edge of the path. Looking over the ledge, there is a long fall down a nearly vertical cliff, to a talus slope of rock pieces that have broken off the top of the mountain, fading into a forest that hides a deep valley far below. As your gaze takes this all in, more wind is pushing you flatter to the ground.

Surrounding mountains have begun to disappear in a greyness of falling snow. It is fast and swirling on the more distant areas that can be seen from here, but it is slowly moving in your direction.

"Now you have to prove your worth again. You got here, now you need to get home again. Thought it was all about the quest, didn't you? Well, even a quest has an end, and a journey home! We aren't going to talk much today. You have a journey to accomplish, and it will be hard. You better get moving before the snow catches you." But snowflakes are already falling.

W IS FOR WORKMANSHIP AND WRITING.

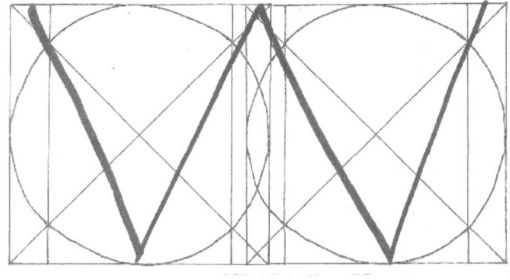

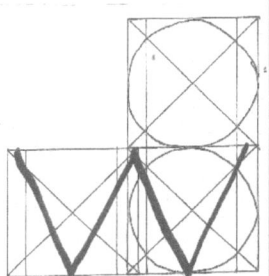

WORKMANSHIP

Carefully go through the steps, using the best skill you have, doing things in the order that is most sensible. Only take the shortcuts that are likely to improve the outcome, and avoid the lazy way out.

WRITING

Every work counts. Every punctuation matters. The words arrange themselves in ways that convey information and emotion, ideas and feelings. And, best of all, writing preserves the thoughts for the future.

WISTERIA

Family: Pea (Fabaceae)

Genus: Wisteria frutescens, American Wisteria

Travel south and you will see wisteria growing wild. This is quite a sight: it loves to climb, and trees are the only real trellis in the woods. So, it climbs the trees. But its weight is enough to pull the tree to the ground. Usually this means breaking the tree.

How do you prune the vine? Southerners will tell you the only way is with a chain saw. Friends have had it planted by the house: but the house was a frame construction and the vine came through the planks and into the interior of the house! Charming to the youth of the family, but a real headache to the adults in charge!

Wisteria is beautiful. If properly grown, it adds grace and beauty to the yard. In an arbor, the path of blooms hanging overhead can be breathtaking.

It is refreshing, in a way, to see such exuberance for life!

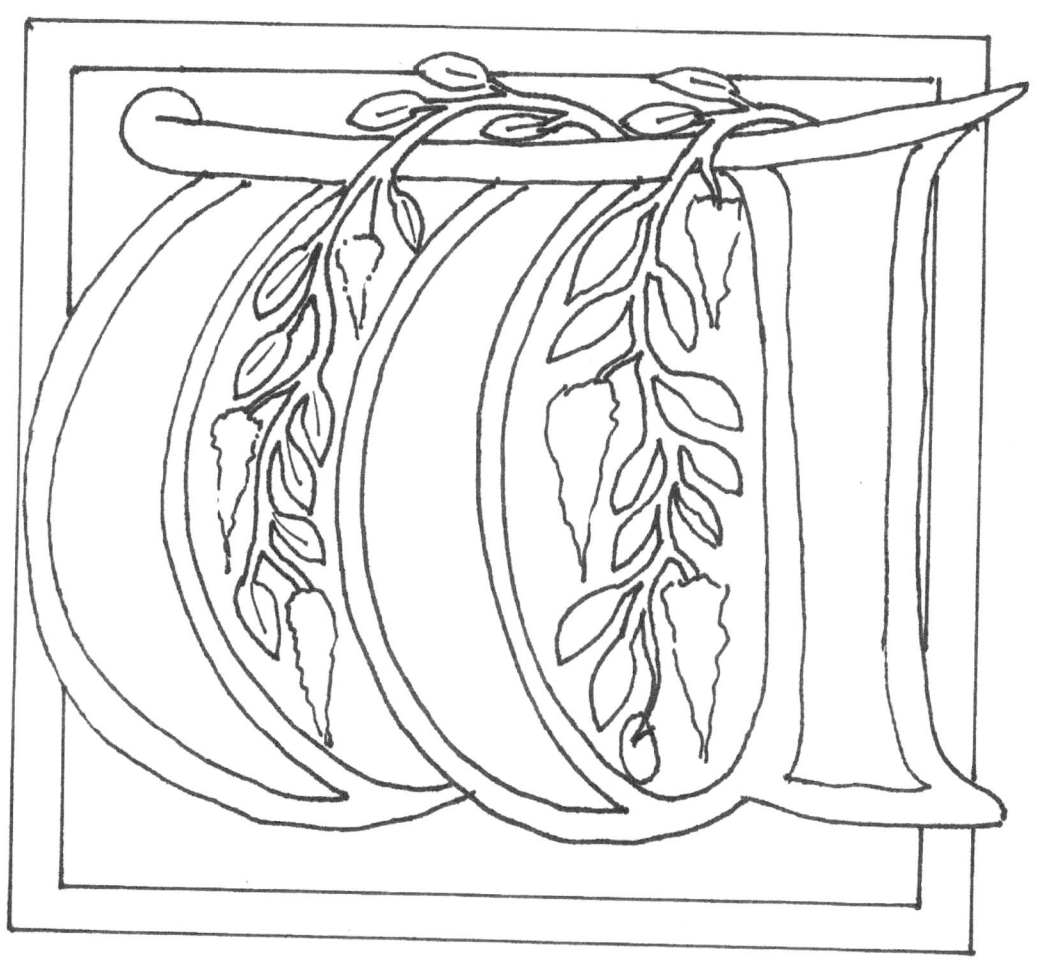

The letter W is associated with Gemini, the twins. It is the Zodiac sign from May 21 to June 20. It is an Air sign ruled by Mercury.

The symbol for Gemini is two standing lines, connected by two horizontal lines, one at top and one at bottom. The W is called a 'double-U' because of its formation with two left loops like the U.

Color choices for Gemini and W include the following. Gemini is orange, and the complementary color is blue. Gemini is ruled by Mercury, which is also orange. It is an Air sign, and the color for Air is yellow.

On the first W, page 183, the diamond shapes can be made with shading. That is done by coloring a diamond really dark at the outline, and getting gradually lighter toward the center. If all the diamonds are done like this, it will look like the background is quilted.

Shading can also be done when two forms overlap. The one on the bottom is shaded as if the one on top were casting a shadow.

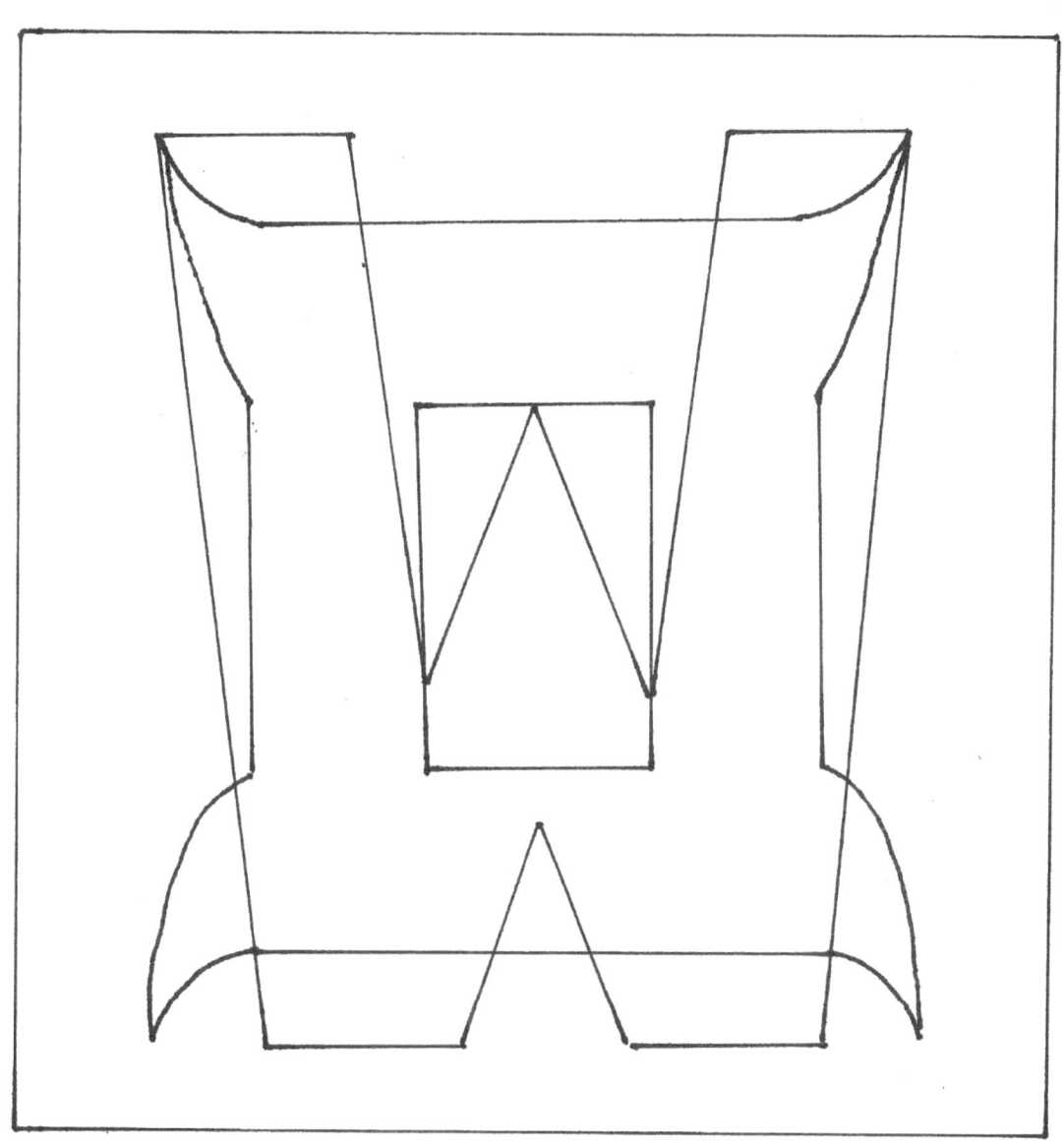

W glances over at you, then continues. "Now, look at me. I have two U's so I already carry an ally along with me! But I suppose you would call that cheating. Oh, well. Anyway. So, you are doing path working journeys. That is good. Let me ask you: how have you been processing the experiences? They are more than just a vacation trip, you know. Each one has things that you can learn, and that is always a good thing. Think of it like this: you get to learn, without having to pay the full tuition in the school of life. Yep. You get to piggyback on someone else's nickel."

The chuckle comes from deep within W's second loop, like a breeze passing through a field of reeds. "All those images you see, all the experiences, they are all ideas. Someone worked hard to assemble the details in a specific way so you would have appropriate experiences. That way, you get to learn something, explore something, try out new things. And there you are, you left your body conveniently back at home. All you need here is your mind. Don't lose that! You need your mind to register and sort the experiences!"

"Here." W hands you a small journal and a pen. "Practice writing down all that you experience on these path workings. And write down everything that those experiences make you think about. Keep a record as skillfully as the construction of that cabin. Every time you create something, that is your goal: make it as skillfully as your current ability allows. Never mind if anyone ever sees it or reads it. just do your best. Oh, to answer your question, that is my home. Visit me there, next time you come to this land, OK?"

"Time for me to go. You can see yourself out. You will know the way, just watch for it." And, as quick as that, W is gone, down to the pier and into the sailboat. Before it registers, W is halfway across the pond, and never looks back.

X IS FOR EXAMPLE AND EXPOSING.

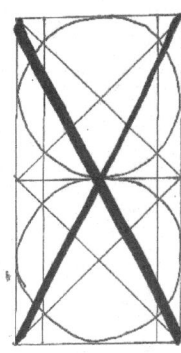

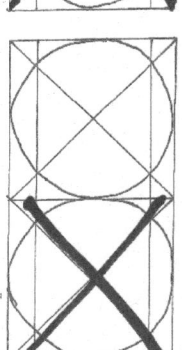

EXAMPLE

There are times when the strict rule must be broken to give a viable result. As an example, the X words use the EX instead of the letter itself. The X section of the dictionary is really short!

EXPOSING

Shine a bright light on things. Look at the issue in the clear light of the sun. let the fresh air clear your mind and show you how things are without the clouds of emotion and doubt.

XANTHIUM

Family: Composite (Compositae)

Genus: Xanthium spinosum, Spiny Clotbur

Well, here is a surprise! If you try to pick it, you will find the spines!

The flowers are not large, and they are not brightly colored. In fact, the whole plant has spines and prickles. The flowers have hooked spines.

Fortunately, this plant like "waste places", which means you are already on guard against the weeds you encounter in such a space.

This plant has the distinction of being one of the few with an X in its name. For that reason, it was chosen to adorn the letter presented here. Enjoy!

The letter X is associated with the Sun. It is most prominent in the summer, but we like seeing it in winter, too, because it makes the snow shine, and is only up a little while. In the summer, though, it is up a lot longer, and makes everything grow. The Sun is an Air planet.

The symbol for the Sun is a sun disk with a bright halo of light around it. the letter X marks the center of our solar system, where the Sun is.

Color choices are in a specific range: The Sun is yellow, and so is Air. Try using different shades, tints or hues of yellow as if they were different colors.

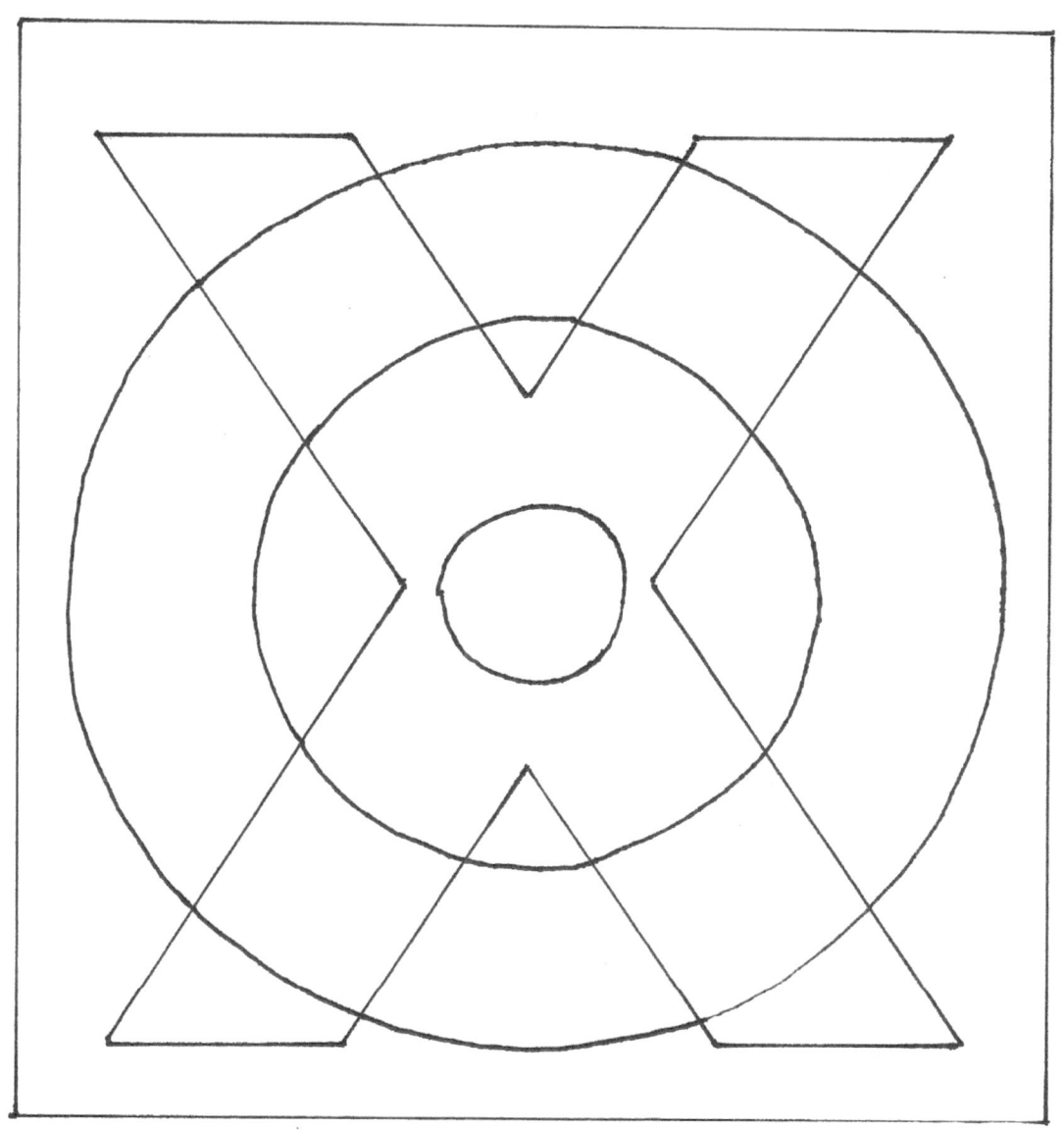

"Welcome to the land of the sun. I see that you are unbalanced, and that cannot stand."

It feels like the gravity is shifting, and it is hard to stay on your feet. "We can work on that."

"Work with opposites. Bounce from day to night, from light to shadow." X moves beside you, and you both face the rising sun. "When I move, there is no shadow. But the shadow is real. Turn around."

You turn, facing away from the sun. "There is your shadow. Any time you are in the light, it is there. It balances you. If you face away from it, you will never have true balance. Accept that. But if you only turn your back to the light, you will be captured by shadow, and never see the light. Balance. All about balance."

X moves and nudges you to also move, so that you are both facing what would be south. "Now you see both the light and the shadow. You reach out one hand to each. Do it. Yes, arms at shoulder height. Look to the left: there is your light. Look to the right: there is your shadow. Feel their weight. It presses your hands down. Which one will win? You need both, neither is better than the other."

"Too much o the light will fry you. You will burn out. Shrivel up like a prune. Become a raisin. You are human, not raisin! You need the light, yes, but it can kill you, too!"

You are getting thirsty; the light of the sun feels heavy on your head and shoulders. It presses you into the ground. It blinds you so that nothing is visible. Looking at the landscape around you, the light is passing through everything like X-rays. The thought is amusing. But there is no definition no differentiation between things. As the light grows, the whole world becomes one white glowing presence.

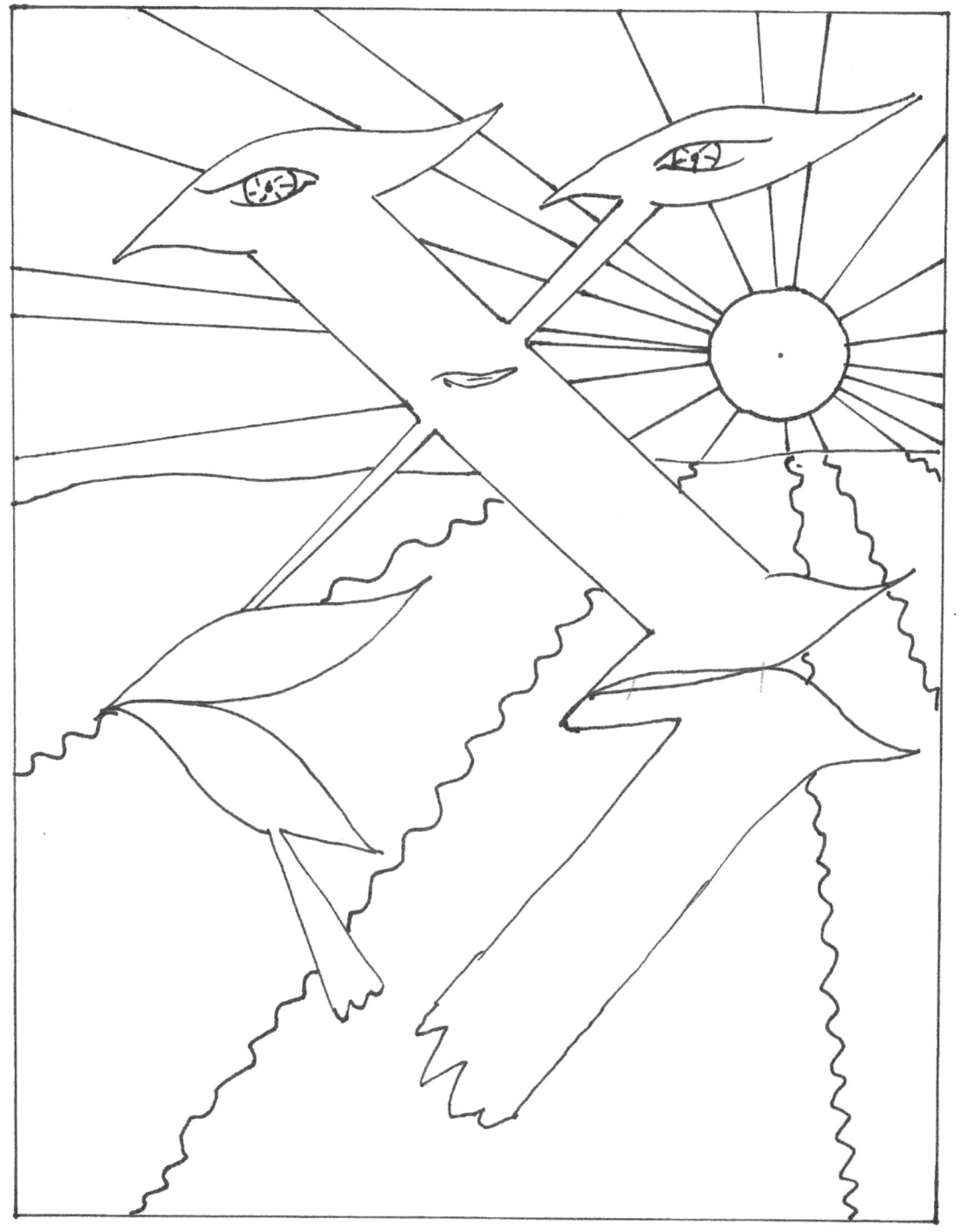

Y IS FOR YIELDING AND YEARNING.

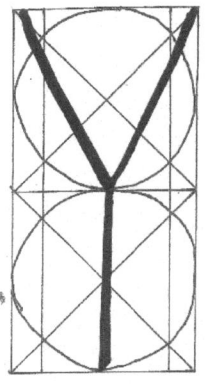

YIELDING

When you yield, only yield to a higher, better or more appropriate alternative. Be strategic, choose when to let opposition have the battle so you can win the war.

YEARNING

Deep desire causes movement. Without the yearned-for outcome, there is dissatisfaction and discontent. Yield to the yearnings of your higher nature. Resist that yearnings of the baser self.

YEW

Family: Yew (Taxaceae)
Genus: Taxus baccata

Yew trees last a very, very long time. They are planted around buildings, but often removed again once they are established. This makes little sense, except that some people favor little snowball bushes, and Yew will grow larger over time. Ah, well! Removing old yew hedges provides a curbside supply of wood for crafters!

Yew may have been the World Tree of the Norse. That is still being discussed by folks who are interested in the authentic translation of traditional literature.

Yew was used for the English longbow, providing a military advantage. Yew bends easily, which saves it in heavy snow. The branches simply bend with the weight.

They are also planted in cemeteries, and have become one of the trees symbolizing death. It is poisonous, except the red flesh on the berries. That kept the cattle away from the cemetery in traditional village life.

Yew likes to be pruned, which makes it ideal for landscaping.

The letter Y is associated with Pisces, the two fish. Its dates are February 20 to March 19, it is a Water sign and is ruled by Jupiter.

The symbol for Pisces is two curves that represent the two fish, with a horizontal line holding them together. In Astronomy, the fish swim in two different directions: one goes north-south; the other goes east-west.

Color choices can include the following.

Pisces is red-violet, or magenta, and its complementary color is yellow-green.

Jupiter's color is blue, and so is water's color.

"You are doing well! Have you done this before? No? Well! Very good, then. Breathing all right? Yes? Good."

A small shrimp swims by, distracting in its lively mode of swimming. "There are a lot of emotions floating around here. What you feel depends on what is going on with you before you visit. There are only a few monsters in the deeper water. You can visit them if you wish. No? Well, maybe not today. But if they disturb you, come back again and deal with them here. It's easier to catch them before they are strong enough to get out of the water. Now, where was I?"

Y turns in a complete circle, then continues. "Oh, yes. If you need to rinse out your mind, come here and flush it off. There are a lot of things you can get up to here. Have you caught up with what is happening in this path? Good. So, we are going to take a tour. There are a few kinds of water here, each has its own uses. As a fish, you can explore all of them. Now? Oh, you are in an ocean mode. Come here."

Again, Y takes your hand and pulls you swiftly through the water, into a calm bay. As you move on to the river that empties into it, your form changes to a fresh-water fish. Still, Y continues into the river, against the current, into a stream. Again, you transform into an air-breather, as a small insect floating on the water of a woodland pool.

Suddenly, you are in the air, this time as a bit of mist. This is a strange feeling, as you are pulled up into a cloud, surrounded by cool whiteness. There you tumble around a bit, then find yourself falling. Y is gone, but it feels natural to fall, and you are a raindrop. As you fall, you see that you are back out in the ocean. But it is riled up now, with seafoam at the crests of huge waves. As you hit the water, you return to a fishlike form. Soon, you find yourself returned to your own self, at home, where you began your journey.

Z IS FOR ZODIAC AND ZONE.

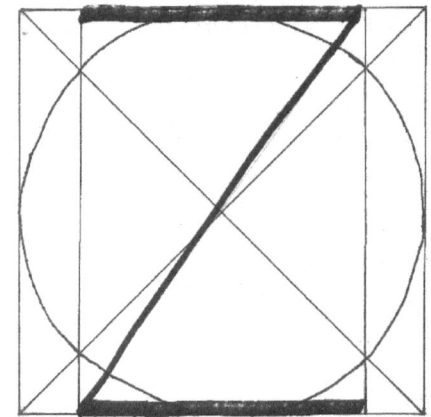

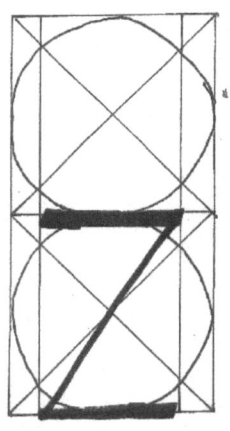

ZODIAC

There are twelve signs in the Zodiac. Each one has a nature based in part on the time of year assigned to it. But, in addition, there are other parts of the sign's natures, beyond the calendar. No one characteristic limits their nature.

ZONE

Limiting the field of our efforts allows us to maximize our skills while limiting exposure to our weaknesses. When we are able to dive in completely, we are in the "zone", a special place of attention and skill that produces the most satisfying results.

ZIZIA

Family: Parsley (Umbelliferae)

Genus: Zizia aurea, Golden Alexanders

In late spring or early summer, driving along country roads, the wild garden will be in full bloom. These are the tallest roadside plant, with chicory and wild carrot and tall white clover blending into a charming treat.

Black swallowtails love the foliage of this plant, giving it added charm. The nectar is a royal feast for the insects of the neighborhood. And its beautiful yellow glow adds to the pleasure on a drive in the country.

The overall shape resembles the wild carrot, the Queen Ann's Lace, but the golden color is unmistakable. It takes a little practice to know the difference between it and the wild parsnip, a close cousin that also grows in open field and wasteland environments.

209

The letter Z is associated with the planet Saturn. This is the gas giant planet that is the furthest from the Sun, at least of the traditional planets. There are more: Pluto, Neptune, and the like. Saturn looks out into deep space, and is the traditional planet of death and rebirth. It is a Watery planet.

The symbol for Saturn is complex. The upper part is a cross that combines the male vertical with the female horizontal. The symbol stands firmly on the vertical stem on the left. Then, an arched curve like a large crescent Moon is on the right side, with a reversed small crescent at the end of the line.

The color choices include the following.

Saturn is sometimes related to indigo, a deep blue that is almost black. This is related to its symbolism in the Magical Qabalah. Deep rust, or better yet, white, are the complementary colors for indigo.

Now, Saturn can be given the color bright rose, or magenta, or red-violet, because that is where it fits in the magical colors (in the Abcedrian System). The complementary color is yellow-green when magenta is used.

Saturn is a Watery planet, and the color of Water is blue.

Her base, instead of being feet, is more like the rocker on a chair on which she is constantly swaying in comforting and rhythmic motion.

You approach, and find yourself held comfortingly by Z. It feels like being held in the arms of a giant Mother, but there are no arms. It is comforting and protecting, and you relax into the warm embrace. If you turn your head slightly you can see the western sky over the sea. It has turned deep rose, and the sun is just at the horizon.

"What you see are the weary souls that have passed out of your physical world. They are so weary! Each one will rest until they are ready for the next steps. You saw some who were already prepared, and they passed up into the Universe, or into the Source of Life, or into eternal life. Each one follows their belief."

As you form the question, Z answers it. "These souls here are resting to regain their vitality and strength, perhaps to plan a little, because they will each move on to another lifetime on your Earth. Look! Some are ready to leave now!"

You look toward the beach, and see a small group of the spirits go up to a small cauldron that is on the edge of the lawn. Each one takes out a set of body parts, and puts it on like a suit of clothing. Then they rush off down the beach, and s they go, they are lifted off the sand to run through the air. In the distance, they round a point, and are gone from view.

"There they go! It is so joyous to see them new and lively! I think that group should do well. They stayed a long time, and are well fortified for their new life. I hope to see them again sone day, returned with stories to tell and memories to process!"

If you find the information in this book to be interesting, there are more detailed books available on some topics covered. This book is intended for anyone who like coloring, especially adults. But information has been put in to keep you interested in the process of moving from letter to letter.

The skeleton alphabet is on the very first page of each letter. This is the form that we all learn as children. It is the pattern we carry in our minds to let us recognize all the derived forms in each font and alphabet. It lets us read the letters in combination with other letters. At the end of the day, this is perhaps the most magical skill we all share: literacy. Cherish it, and practice it.

On the same page, two interesting words have been described that begin with the letter you are coloring. These words are the Abcedrian words: that is why they begin with the letter. Why are they used? To focus on characteristics associated with the letter in that system. They describe the Zodiac, planet or element that the letter is associated with.

The first design in each set uses a "Black letter" form, placed over a diaper pattern. This is traditional: but you do not need to stick to tradition to choose your colors!

Next, a plant is described. There is no special significance to the choice of plant, other than to make sure the name begins with the letter it is depicted with. The letter itself is a Versal Capital, used with late medieval manuscripts.

The third design is called a "flashing letter". As mentioned, every letter is associated with astrology/alchemy as a Zodiac sign, planet or element. Here, the traditional symbol is overlapped with the letter, both being drawn as block letters. This creates a checkerboard pattern that can be colored with contrasting colors. Complementary colors, when pure and solid, tend to vibrate in the eye: it makes the letter and symbol flash in and out of focus.

The final design is a cartoon of the letter, in an environment suggested in the reading opposite it. The reading is extracted from the path working meditations found in "Traveling the Triple Septagram" by the same author as this book.

If you are interested in this magical approach to the alphabet, we can suggest the books that describe the whole system: "The Abcedrian System" for the overview of the system; "Traveling the Triple Septagram" for the path working meditations; "Working in the Spheres"; and "Meeting the Planets", another coloring book. All are from Lulu.com, on Amazon.com, and other sources, and are written by the author of this book.